#PRAY LIVE WIN

"The title of a sermon I recently heard came to mind as I read the pages of this book – "What You Gonna Do?" Sisters begin your journey right now searching first for God's divine will and purpose in everything you do. Don't wait another minute relying on your own strengths and intuitions. Allow this book to be your guide. Dee has demonstrated in her own life these written words!"

> – Rev. Regena L. Thomas, Pastor Allen AME Church
> Atlantic City, NJ and Former New Jersey Secretary of State

"Dee Marshall, doing what she does through her motivating words and powerful prayers, will move you from an average to an abundant prayer life. This book shows us how to step up and pray up! #PrayLiveWin gives great insight and ignites your winning spirit as you journey to all God has created you to be."

> – Yolanda Carroll, Co-Pastor Abundant Love
> Christian Center, Houston, TX

"#PrayLiveWin is an "Aha" moment that challenged me to check myself on several fronts, while at the same time inspired me that I can be my best self through the power of prayer and an unrelenting faith in God. Thank you, thank you, thank you for the honor of getting a sneak peak of your transforming gift for the ages – #PrayLiveWin. It will change lives."

> – Melanie L. Campbell, President & CEO, National
> Coalition on Black Civic Participation & Convener,
> Black Women's Roundtable

"In #PrayLiveWin …a prayer resource for women, Dee Marshall uses just the right blend of scripture, life experience and exhortation to challenge women to do life decently and in order. She reminds us that we are made in God's image and privy to the many resources that He has provided. Straight talk for crooked times is my best description for this insightful tool."

— *Tawana Ford Sabbath, MSS, Ph.D., Philadelphia, PA*

"If you are early in your Christian walk and trying to figure out what to talk to God about – and why and how – this book is for you. If you have been walking with the Lord for a while but you long for deeper intimacy with Him and right-now awareness of His work in your life, this book is for you. If the Christian walk is "a long obedience in the same direction," this book is a guide for women who understand they must make that walk with their hand firmly in the hand of the Lord."

— *Debra Stewart, Houston, TX*

"Dee Marshall, you are an amazing women of God, and we as people living in the Kingdom are excited about what you are doing and what you are about to do. Someone owning this book can be compared to them having prayer attached to their lives daily. You are truly a blessing and the WORLD is waiting on you. With much love and respect."

— *Kingdom Alive Magazine*

"In this book Sis. Dee Marshall reintroduces to a desperate world, the hinge on the door that opens up answers to all of life's questions – prayer. This book will teach you and talk to you about who you are, and then position you to walk in the fullness of the promises of God. Enjoy reconnecting with our Great God, Greatness! :)"

– *Dr. Maria Seaman, Senior Pastor Shekinah Worship Center,*
Bermuda

"The Bible says the earnest prayer of a righteous person has great power and produces wonderful results.(James 5:16b NLT) Dee Marshall has made it a priority to teach and encourage others to pray. If you want a wonderful life, learn to pray. Thank you Dee for helping us to overcome our fear, lack of desire, and ambivalence to prayer, by reminding us daily that we can pray."

– *Pastor Mia Wright, Co Pastor, The Fountain of Praise*
Houston, TX

"#PrayLiveWin is a must read for every person of faith, regardless of where they are on their spiritual journey. #PrayLiveWin is written in a fresh, relatable God-breath voice. Dee Marshall has generously poured out the living water on paper, gifting readers a timeless tool to experience the power of prayer in any season."

– *Norma L. Jarrett, Essence Magazine Bestselling Author*

"When you pray and live you will win every time!!! This book will be an asset to your life. iBelieve."

– *Pastor Mary Searight, Abundant Life Family Worship*
Center, New Brunswick, NJ

"God has used Dee Marshall to literally change the lives of thousands of women by reinforcing the power of prayer. Healing deliverance and empowerment are happening all over the world for women and their families because of "Girlfriends Pray". I am blessed to be one of those women. I know #PrayLiveWin will be just as impactful."

– Donna Soaries, First Lady of First Baptist Church
of Lincoln Gardens, Somerset, NJ

"We've all been there—in the valley—when we didn't know where to turn, what to say, what to do. Dee Marshall knows, beyond the shadow of a doubt, the answer is prayer. A motivational life coach and spiritual warrior, Dee has written this powerful book to offer comfort and joy to women everywhere. Whatever the problem, she offers a prayer, then backs it up with proof in the scriptures. Glory to God for this most awesome work!"

– Monique Greenwood, Author of Having What Matters
and Owner & CEO (Chief Enjoyment Officer)
of Akwaaba Bed & Breakfast Inns

"You can always count on Dee Marshall to deliver a timely prayer that's sure to reach heaven. Her prayers are poignant, refreshing, uplifting, honest, and direct. I encourage women everywhere to use the heartfelt prayers in #PrayLiveWin in their daily walk with God."

– Lori George Billingsley, Atlanta, GA

#PRAY LIVE WIN

52 PRACTICAL PRAYERS FOR WOMEN

DEE C. MARSHALL

Raise The Bar, LLC.
© Copyright 2015 by Dee C. Marshall

ISBN-13: 978-0692401804 (Custom Universal)
ISBN-10: 0692401806

Library of Congress Control Number: 2015903835
CreateSpace Independent Publishing Platform, North Charleston, SC

BISAC: Religion / Prayerbooks / Christiann

In Memory of
Terry Charmaine Pinder – My Aunt TT
one of my biggest fans
who won't get to see the book,
touch the pages or feel my love
or the presence of God unfold here.

xoxo

Acknowledgements

To my Emmy... Thank you for being an awesome mom, supporter, and silent partner; advising on everything from make-up, hair, wardrobe, and the book cover.

To my Father... Thank you for showing me the discipline of prayer.

To Granny... Thank you for praying for me and gifting me my most valuable asset to date: my *NIV Women's Devotional Bible* that caught my tears, heard my cries and fueled my faith to follow and to serve God in a big way.

To my biggest cheerleaders who "knew me when" and watched me grow... God Mom, Juice, Aunt B, Aunt Swolly, and Aunt Nancy, I thank God for you.

To my girls... Rhonda, Michellene, Theo, Nik, Yolanda, Teresa and Marilyn, I appreciate you all for being good friends, prayer partners, and awesome cheerleaders.

To my road management – The Soulcial Butterfly Agency... Stefani, I thank God He allowed our paths to cross right when I needed your services and extra love and care to support me as I move around the globe about my Father's business.

To my "Get-er-Done" Dawn Jordan Jones... Thank you for being a "tee-tee" to this book when I, at the twelfth hour, could do no more.

To my mentors and friends for over a decade: my Pastor Reverend DeForest Soaries, Jr. and Donna Soaries... I thank you for trusting me to serve and be a part of your vision; teaching me so much during my time with you. That was not a job but more like a "paid internship" that brought me to this point.

To my Sunday School teacher ... Thank you Sister Tawana for the gift of your teaching and for being an instrument to further stretch my knowledge of our Lord and Savior.

To my Girlfriends Pray Team... I thank God for you: Ordinary women committed to doing the extraordinary work to move towards the vision of one million women.

To my Girlfriends Pray Ambassadors... I thank God for sending you "Foot Soldiers" to go out and serve the masses in this capacity.

To my Girlfriends Pray Life Camp... I love you JGs and I thank you for allowing me to serve you and support the next best version of who God called you to be.

To the Girlfriends Pray Board of Directors and Advisory Board...I am so grateful you believed in the vision God gave me and choose to run alongside to reach the masses.

Introduction

BEFORE WE BEGIN OUR 52-WEEK JOURNEY OF PRAYING, living (abundantly,) and winning, there is something I need to share with you.

God has positioned me in a way that my primary day-to-day work involves using my gift to coach women. I am told I am pretty good at it, and I do believe that God has given me an innate ability to speak life into the lives of women and to equip them to go higher. But I am not the first resource in figuring out life's issues. The truth is God is the true Go-to-Guide for figuring out life, no matter how big or small, difficult or embarrassing the issue.

I am only a vessel, allowing myself to be used by God to do His work and speak through me. So I spend most of my days advising women on how to live their best life by sharing best practices, tips, tools and strategies on how to live and win. I find no greater joy than when women discover, once and for all, who God created them to be and when they find their purpose in life. However, my first piece of advice to women (and all people, for that matter) is to listen to what God has to say about your situation, and trust His voice over your girlfriend's, spouse's, mother's, father's, sister's or brother's. Trust God's Word over your most trusted confidante, your Pastor, therapist, and even me.

I wrote this book first for Girlfriends Pray and for our local prayer groups located in four countries around the world. My message is simple: seek God first about everything. Share with God every silly thing, every shameful and painful dark moment, and every embarrassing encounter. Ask God to direct you to the right resources that will speak into your life, and He will either send people your way or point you towards a means to assist you. But either way, you've got to trust Him on the timing and the vessels He assigns to serve and support you. As human beings we are sold on needing to hear someone else in the natural. We like for an audible voice of flesh-and-bone people we can see ☺... to give us advice, direction, guidance and insight on life matters. And though it is sometimes comforting, I encourage you to reconsider that reflex and make sure God is your first counselor. Anyone else will simply serve as confirmation for what God is resolving in your spirit. Wherever there is peace, there is God. Your answer from God is there if you listen. It is your firm resolve.

Psalm 32:8 says, "For I shall teach you; I shall make known to you the way in which to go and I shall set my eyes upon you." In other words, God says, *I will give you direction on what to do.* So do not move too fast, but pay attention when God is showing up by way of a nudging in your spirit. Seek Him and tune in to how your spirit is feeling and/or responding. God is your first and immediate go-to for direction on what to do, how to handle, how to respond, resolve, and address every situation. I have known God to show up in two ways. You can seek Him for His will when the answer is not present. Or, if and when you don't hear from Him, it is probably that He has already spoken on the matter and He is just waiting on you to act on His command.

A lot of times, we are looking for God to speak right now in the moment and I believe He's thinking, *"Didn't you hear me the first time? I wrote it in the Word, daughter, and I have directed you to truth which is my word.* "All Scripture is breathed out by God and profitable for teaching, for reproof, for correction, and for training in righteousness, that the man of God may be competent, equipped for every good work." (2 Timothy 3:16-17) But we either don't know the Word, or, if we do know the Word, many of us do not follow the Word even though it is written in black and white.

Listen up, Greatness. The Bible is our life manual. It is our instruction manual, our curriculum for life, and a playbook if you want to win. It tells us everything we need to know about who we are. Think of a household product like a blender. A blender comes with a manufacturer's instruction manual. If you wanted to know how it worked, you wouldn't consult the blender. You would consult the manufacturer (the creator of the blender.) Now, you may be thinking, "I already know how a blender works." But therein lies the problem. We think we know, but the truth is, we have *no* idea! We don't know everything and we are too quick to make assumptions. We just plug it in and start pushing buttons on the blender without looking at the manual...until there's a malfunction and the kitchen suddenly smells like smoke. The truth of the matter is, you would never know the full capacity of the blender or how it's made until you read the manual.

In the same way, if you want to figure out what you are made of, and what you are purposed to do, then you must turn to your Creator, the Manufacturer of your life. What you may not realize is that the Word of God is filled with such yummy stuff to address our needs, wants, desires, issues and challenges. It's all there, and in some instances, just knowing what God has to say about a situation will calm your nerves and resolve your fears.

The Word of God answers life's most challenging situations. And life works so much better when you have a relationship with the Author. God will not only speak from the pages, but He will also make His word a reality in your heart so that the answers are firm, and you no longer question whatever situation He resolves for you. When God makes the Word a reality in your heart, you will have a personal experience; and through that experience, you will be compelled to go deeper in your walk with the Lord.

If you've never read the instruction manual for the blender, it may work for a while, but there is a great chance you will misuse it or break it. You will never get your money's worth if you are not using it at its full capacity. In the same way, when we don't follow the manual laid out for our lives, we, too, become less effective in our purpose. We become frustrated and distracted all because we aren't functioning at 100%. And why aren't we functioning at 100%? Because we didn't consult, read, or obey the Word of God.

I say that to say, since you came with a manual, use it! There is no need to struggle in life forever. The Word says "… I've come that they may have life and have it to the full" (John 10:10) and it is not God's intention for you to live in a constant state of struggle, wandering in the wilderness.

Nothing happens until you decide to relocate from the land of lack to a place of abundance. God is the God of more than enough. He promised us a plan for our lives and that plan is to prosper us (Jeremiah 29:11.) If that's your desire, then you must look at the manual and make up in your mind that today will be your last day of living average. Today will be the last day you live without the manual. Make up your mind that today you will turn a new corner and begin to seek God first on all matters, big and small. Then commit to applying the Word to your life!

It took me less than thirty days to get this book on paper. The data dumped from my head onto these pages, and it happened vis-a-vis a supernatural flow from God. There's no other way to explain it. Because of that, I say to you, God must be up to something amazing in your life! He wanted you to have this. So please don't let my efforts … our efforts be in vain. I speak to your potential and demand that you step up and pray up! Watch God do a supernatural work in your life.

Father God, thank you for choosing me to birth this book. Thank you for using me in spite of me. I pray for a decrease in me that you might increase in these pages that I would be but a vessel for you to speak to your daughters directly and shift the atmosphere in every space they occupy so their lives would be blessed in every way. I pray every bystander witnessing and watching her would see you in her as a result of her pressing into you in prayer. I love you, Lord. I thank you. I praise you… In Jesus' Name, I seal this prayer and leave it at your feet. Amen. Dee J ☺

How to use this book

THIS IS A STANDALONE PRAYER RESOURCE THAT YOU MAY run to when you are going through some of life's everyday challenges. This book is not intended to be an extensive and comprehensive bible study on prayer. Rather, it is a guide for marrying the natural with the spiritual. In other words, it is intended to be a focused prayer reference to address your real life stuff right now. It's intended to connect the dots of your life by pulling down the Scriptures so that your natural needs will be met with spiritual application.

Remember, prayer is a conversation with God. As such, He requires us to be in conversation with Him if we want to have a relationship with Him. It's a conversation; therefore there is no right or wrong way to pray. In order to access God, however, we must believe in Him (Hebrews 11:6) before we can come to Him. There is a model prayer known as "the Lord's Prayer" but it's really the Disciples Prayer. It's found in the gospels where the disciples ask Jesus "Lord, teach us how to pray." (Luke 11:1) They had caught wind of the fact that Jesus would randomly go off and come back with what seemed like some super human ability... so the disciples didn't ask Jesus to teach us how to perform miracles (i.e. heal the sick, make the blind see, bring people back to life, multiply the fish and five loaves, etc..) They said "Hold up, hold up, hold up! Jesus teach us that!" That's what you ought to do. Ask the Lord to teach you how to pray because when Jesus prayed and pressed into the Father's presence, He was fueled, filled, enabled, anointed.... and all that.

As you use this book as a go-to resource to pray about a specific life need, want, desire, challenge, issue, situation or circumstance, realize that because of the Holy Spirit within you, you have direct access to God through your own prayer. When reading the book, I encourage you to focus on a single chapter for seven days even though it may take you fifteen minutes to read it. Seven is the number of completion. Seven is the number of days it took God to complete the cycle of creating a masterpiece in the earth so I always encourage seven day emergence and not to move so quickly. Focus and connect the dots in the Word of God and whatever you are receiving from God, stand boldly by it (Hebrews 4:16.) Believe that our Lord and Savior will show up, because He will!

Take one chapter at a time. Read through the motivation deposit first, and then read the prayer. Then, spend a few minutes every day for seven days as follows:

(a) In quiet time, praying about it.

(b) In quiet time, journaling about it. (Let your thoughts and feelings flow freely.)

(c) In quiet time, conducting your own Bible search (the topic) and study.

(d) Before you go to bed, confess your situation to the Lord. Then, go to sleep and wait for God's response no matter how long it takes for Him to respond. (Psalm 5:3)

READ WITH A PRAYER OR ACCOUNTABILITY PARTNER

Find a friend, colleague, co-worker or family member to journey with you. Gift a copy of this book to them. Then ask them to agree to hold you accountable by committing to a weekly email, telephone call, or Skype conversation. Or by perhaps conduct in a live connect meeting at a bookstore, coffee shop, park, spa, and beach, wherever you feel most comfortable. Your accountability connection can be a 30-minute block of time where each person shares for 15 minutes, or you can decide what works best for each of you. The goal is to stay committed, consistent and supportive of each other. Never give up on yourself or your partner.

READ WITH A PRAYER OR ACCOUNTABILITY GROUP

Join a Girlfriends Pray Local group for access to live support meetings, food, fun and fellowship in a healthy loving environment with other women of faith. We offer a little more structure and resources to support you along your spiritual walk. Visit www.GirlfriendsPray.org to find a group in your area. If there are no groups in your immediate area, consider starting a group. Details are available on our website.

Table of Contents

1
A prayer for
the journey

> "Now to Him who is able to do far more abundantly
> beyond all that we ask or think, according to the
> power that works within us..."
> — **Ephesians 3:20 ESV**

"GOD'S BLESSINGS ARE CHASING ME DOWN."
I remember posting these words to my Facebook status a short time ago. It was during a season where I felt "overwhelmed" by the favor of God on my life. His blessings were continuous. So much so, that I was living in a state of awe at how He would show up over, and over, and over again. In fact, the blessings were so constant, in the back of my mind I was in slight disbelief. I remember this one moment when I allowed an itty bit of fear to intrude on my thoughts. Though faint (and thankfully fleeting,) I thought "This can't go on forever, the way God is blessing me." However, I have come to discover that this is *exactly* the kind of life God intended for me. And for you.

When you live for God, I mean really live for Him and follow Him wholly, His favor on your life will be steadfast and relentless. His love endures forever and the manifestation of His love will show up in your everyday walk with Him. This, woman of God, is how the winning in life happens and what it looks like.

When you surrender to living your life fully, completely, 24/7, and not just on Sundays like a surface-level Christian, God has no choice but to see your faith and respond in kind. In Mark 2:4, I'm fascinated by the lame man whose friends pressed their way toward Jesus with the total expectation that Jesus would heal him. The lame man's friends cut a hole through the roof of where Jesus was hanging out. *That* is faith. You have to allow God to see you coming through the roof! That gesture would demonstrate that you, too, have fully surrendered; that despite obstacles in your path, you have found a bold way to press forward to be in His presence. The lame man was healed because of his faith and boldness. There is no doubt in my mind that when you chase God down like that, He will chase you down and bless your obedience. This is where the winning begins: by chasing Him down.

If you are going through a season in your life, where you feel as if God has forgotten about you, doesn't love you, or is angry at you, please understand that's not the nature of God. God loves you and wants the best for you. His word says in John 10:10, "I've come that they may have life and have it to the full." He's talking about you. God came to save you and because He saved you; purchased you with a price, He owns you. Since God owns you, it would make sense that He considers you a prized possession that He holds in His palm. And since you are His prized possession, it would also make sense that *He went through the trouble of sacrificing His son for you because He has a plan for your life.* God made a sacrifice for your life and second salvation, and the promise of an eternal life. He came that you would have life to the full, not lacking in anything.

This is why it does *not* make sense that you, a child of the Most High, would live in perpetual seasons of struggle, lack, and defeat; broken in a pit. This is also why it does not make sense for you to go on wandering in circles in the wilderness of life – day after day, month after month, year after year – seeing and doing the same things and getting the same results. Christ came to give you an abundant life! No matter what your situation or circumstances are right now, it is written in Jeremiah 29:11 that God's plan is *to prosper you, give you hope and a future.* You may not believe it yet, but I'm going to believe God to stir up something in you right now; to call your attention to a new possibility and an opening season of perpetual wins. Get into position right now and pray for this journey. God's about to hit it out of the park!

I come to you Jehovah Shalom
The Lord Our Peace
(Judges 6:24)

Father God, in the name of Jesus, I come to you right now to say thank you for the gift of your Son, Jesus. Thank you for life, breath and strength. Thank you for being the head of my life and for sending me this resource to change my life. I boldly declare my intent is to grow closer to you through the discipline of conversation with you. My intent is to increase my prayer life and to seek you for all things. My intent is to be more obedient in presenting everything to you; big and small. Teach me how to give you everything and teach me how to trust you for guidance before I move too swiftly on life matters.

Thank You, God, for forgiving me, covering me, protecting me, leading me and guiding me. You know what I need before I ask. You created me and the plan for my life. For that, I am grateful. You have given me your word that you would bless and prosper me. For that, I am grateful. You have given me your promise of an abundant life! For that, I say, Hallelujah! You think so highly of me and speak such kind words, and with that I want to learn to do the same for myself. God, I want more of you; so fill every vacant space in me. I want what you want for me; so reveal your hidden plan and answers for my life. I want to be who you have created me to be; so change, transform, stretch me and grow me up into a mature Christian and follower of you. Open my heart and attune my ears to your mouth. Speak, Lord. Guide, Lord. Show me, Lord, the way. Draw me nearer to You, Lord. Make it plain. I want to hear what you have to say about my needs, desires, wants, issues, challenges, situations and circumstances.

I seal this prayer in Jesus' Name (John 14:13.) Amen.

If you abide in me, and my words abide in you, ask whatever you wish, and it will be done for you. – John 15:7

Therefore I tell you, whatever you ask in prayer, believe that you have received it, and it will be yours. – Mark 11:24

And I tell you, ask, and it will be given to you; seek, and you will find; knock, and it will be opened to you. – Luke 11:9

Likewise the Spirit helps us in our weakness. For we do not know what to pray for as we ought, but the Spirit himself intercedes for us with groaning's too deep for words. – Romans 8:26

Call to me and I will answer you, and will tell you great and hidden things that you have not known. – Jeremiah 33:3

2
A prayer for better

"I have told you these things, that my joy and delight may
be in you, and that your joy and gladness may be of full
measure and complete and overflowing."
– John 15:11 AMP

M

Y INTENTION FOR WRITING THIS BOOK IS THAT YOU
WOULD read it, pray the prayers, grow closer to God and
have a deeper relationship with Him. However, when I asked myself the question "what do you want for the reader?" I wrote this
book so that you could feel better. Believe it or not, that is the
absolute truth. I started out writing the book out of need and because my life's work is assigned to encouraging women through
prayer. So I was led to package a resource to reach the masses.
However, when I asked myself the question again "what do you
want women to walk away with?" in my heart, I had a solid,
sound and simple resolve. I really want you to feel better NOW as
you read this book and the other things will happen. I want you
to know and accept that God is with you and He is for you and He
has an awesome plan for your life.

Our God in heaven, the Lily of the valley, Mary's baby, the
Author and Finisher of our lives, the One who sits high and looks
low, has your back. I believe reading this book will lead you to
pray about simple things and significant things, little things and

big things and all things in between. If you are led to pray and you pray with a sincere heart, having confessed Jesus the Christ as your personal savior, then God will show up and it's impossible for you not to feel better in the presence of God. The Lord "comforts us in all our affliction" (2 Corinthians 1:4.) Be comforted in this unequivocal truth: God is your Creator, so He holds the plan for your life in His hand. Be comforted knowing that God is your source and supply; God is your covering and protection; God is your hiding place; God fights your battles and defends your case. He settles every judgment against you.

He is God.

And the mere fact that you have access to Him should calm your worries and anxieties. If you read Isaiah 40:1-31 you will hear God reminding us just how sovereign He really is. *Who can compare to God? He says, "Do you not know? Have you not heard? Has it not been told you from the beginning? Have you not understood since the earth was founded? He sits enthroned above the circle of the earth, and its people are like grasshoppers. He stretches out the heavens like a canopy, and spreads them out like a tent to live in."* God is God! He is bigger than your issues, larger than your problems, greater than your needs, and mightier than your circumstances. Just reading that encourages my heart.

With every page you read, I just want you to feel better. So I remind you today, in this moment, that God is your peace. Many of us go through perpetual cycles of defeat and brokenness, and many women are unhappy, unfulfilled, stressed and hopeless. But you have to shake that off! God is your peace. Greatness, let me drop this in your spirit. You don't have to live the way you are living. You are a daughter of the King. You are a child of the highest God, an Heiress to the Throne. Your Daddy in Heaven owns everything and rules everything. You are here on purpose for a purpose. There is a plan for your life. "For I know the plans I have for you, declares the LORD, plans to prosper you and not to harm you, plans to give you hope and a future." (Jeremiah 29:11) Be encouraged in the Word of God, increase your faith by reading it daily because the word of God is truth. It is sound and reliable. It is firm and unmovable. God keeps His promises and if He promised you hope in Jeremiah 29, stand on that word. Believe that. Receive that. Own that. The hallmark of a believer is that we have hope. God is bigger than whatever issue is weighing on your heart. He is able to bring you out of whatever you are in right now.

I come to you God of Comfort
(John 14:26)

Father, in the name of Jesus, I come to you right now confessing that in You, I have my living, my breathing and my being. I thank you for this moment when I can come to you, talk to you and be heard, helped and healed. I surrender my emotional state to you right now. I don't feel 100% but I want to be better. I want a better life but right now my immediate desire is to feel better. My life, my work, my home, my money, my relationships, my health and so many other things weigh so heavily on my spirit that I feel weak and fragile. Nevertheless, Your Word says, "Do not be anxious about anything, but in every situation, by prayer and petition, with thanksgiving, present your requests to God." (Philippians 4:6) So I come to you to thank you for life, breath and strength. I thank you for another day. I thank you that I have a God to call on.

Lord, forgive me for anything I may have done to displease you. Help me to see the errors of my ways and what you require of me. Lord, I don't want anything blocking my access to you; so hear me and know my heart.

Now would you begin to move right now in my spirit? God, I welcome the Spirit to dwell in me and lighten my load, my path and my life. I believe You, Father, are the lifter of my head (Psalm 3:3.) So lift it now and help me to walk upright. Help me to no longer carry every issue, every hurt, every pain, and every disappointment. I give it to You, God. I leave it all here at your feet, and I trust that you have already worked everything out for my good. (Romans 8:28) This is my prayer to you. In Jesus' Name. Amen.

But you, LORD, are a shield around me, my glory, and the one who lifts up my head. – Psalm 3:3

The Lord is on my side; I will not fear. What can man do to me? The Lord is on my side as my helper; I shall look in triumph on those who hate me. It is better to take refuge in the Lord than to trust in man. It is better to take refuge in the Lord than to trust in princes. – Psalm 118:6-9

Fear not, for I am with you; be not dismayed, for I am your God; I will strengthen you, I will help you, I will uphold you with my righteous right hand. – Isaiah 41:10

For I know that through your prayers and the help of the Spirit of Jesus Christ this will turn out for my deliverance. – Philippians 1:19

And I will ask the Father, and he will give you another Helper, to be with you forever. – John 14:16

3
A prayer when you're ready to give up

> "Let us not become weary in doing good, for at the proper
> time we will reap a harvest if we do not give up."
> **– Galatians 6:9**

ONE THING THAT BOTH FRUSTRATES AND SADDENS ME AT the same time is hearing women give up. We have so many women in our communities who are broke, broken, hurt and lost and sadly we are responsible in most of those circumstances. I know this to be true because I've been there myself. Although I've never given up, I know what it feels like to be broke, broken, hurt and hurting. Now that I'm on the other side of struggle and serving women through the ministry, I see it from a different perspective. I see standing on top of struggle as a result of both faith and action. I now know for sure that it is possible to move beyond struggle.

In my ministry, we get tons of correspondence every day from women all over the world. The mail comes in from several different sources including my personal email, my Facebook mail and our Girlfriends Pray Facebook mail. Although we have an awesome team who manages the mail and answers every inquiry, on occasion I check the mail and see their desperate cries for prayer. These are women dealing with life issues (small and large, some serious and some comical, like the woman who wanted to pray for a dog whom we thought was her son.) In any event, they are seeking prayer and they are at the point of giving up, but what they are experiencing is nothing we've never seen or heard of before.

We've had women ready to give up on cheating husbands, women who wanted to give up on their marriage, mothers wanting to give up on drug addicted children, children wanting to give up on ill and aging parents, women wanting to give up on their jobs, homeless women wanting to give up on the system— you name it, we've read it. We've had young women wanting to give up because of dysfunctional living arrangements with parents and so much more. I'll never forget this one woman wanted to give up on life. She sent me an email, and after reading it, I sighed deeply and just shook my head. The best way to explain my feeling at that moment is to be transparent with you. I was more frustrated and disappointed than anything. Her message went something like this...

"... Dear Dee, I am so overwhelmed right now. I need help because I cannot take it anymore. I don't make enough money and the thing that is unbearable is the amount of debt I'm in and the fact that bill collectors keep calling me every day. My phone is ringing off the hook and I just can't take it. I want to kill myself because I don't know what else to do."

Now she was reaching out for help at a time of desperation. But my immediate reaction did not come from a place of empathy but a place of inquiry. Where was her faith? What did she hope in? You see, it's impossible to have faith in God and to have lost all hope at the exact same time. How could you give up faith, give up on God, give up on life because of pressure from bill collectors? It all boils down to pressure of bill collectors calling and that was the breaking point.

Let me drop this in your spirit, Greatness. If you are a woman of faith, if you believe in God and if you believe He is your personal Savior, then understand the hallmark of a believer's hope. As long as you live, you have a promise from God. God has a plan and a purpose for your life. His plan is bigger than what you are going through. You have to have faith throughout every season. And the good news is, all you need is a little faith the size of a mustard seed (Luke 17:6.) When you don't have faith or you demonstrate signs of weak faith, you cancel your prayer. In Matthew 17, the disciples ask Jesus why they weren't seeing results. Jesus said because you have no faith. Think about it. How in the world can you ask God for something if you don't believe in the source? You literally cancel your request to God by sending a mixed message. On the one hand, you are calling yourself a believer. But when the pressures of life arise, you don't believe. Mixed messages will bring about mixed results.

In order for God to deliver you from what you are going through, you must believe God and never see your situation as bigger than God's ability. God can handle your needs but not when you throw in the towel and give up so easily. Firm up your faith and speak to these bills, this debt, this addiction, this judgment, this lawsuit, this illness---none of it is outside of God's reach. God can fix what you can't handle. In fact, He's enabled you to deal with it as well and whatever is beyond your ability is His sweet spot!

Don't be so weak in faith. The enemy comes to steal your joy and kill your spirit and your livelihood. He uses life's struggles to get in your head and tell you lies. The enemy looks for the weak and your weakness is like a welcome mat. "Your enemy the devil prowls around like a roaring lion looking for someone to devour" (1 Peter 5:8.) When you are ready to give up, that's when the enemy has just about won you over to his team. When you are ready to give up, the enemy gets you to look at what you are going through as if you have no hope. When you are broken and over-whelmed, that is when you are the most vulnerable. That is when you are tempted to turn your back on God and speak out against the very thing you asked God for. Giving up implies you have lost hope. But God's answer to your struggle is "rejoice in hope, be patient in tribulation, be constant in prayer" (Romans 12:12.)

I come to You God of Hope
(Titus 2:14)

Father, in the name of Jesus, I come to you right now confessing I have not been faithful. In a weak moment of hardship struggling with [name it _____] I have allowed the enemy to convince me out of hoping in you. I have allowed the enemy to persuade me into giving up. I have overestimated my situation and underestimated your strength. Forgive me. In a moment of confusion and exhaustion, my perception was skewed or, rather, my distance from you left an open door for the enemy.

So I declare right now, you God are greater and bigger than my struggle. (Luke 10:19) The enemy has no power over me and I resist every thought and idea that doesn't line up with your Word of hope. I resist every thought of despair that would try to break forth in my thinking and my speaking. I declare and decree that I will speak the answer and not the problem. I praise you for reminding me of your word in Jeremiah 32:27 "I am the LORD, the God of all humankind. There is, indeed, nothing too difficult for me." I thank you for your promise to give me hope and a future. I thank you Lord for your promise to give me a rich and rewarding life, not lacking in anything (John 10:10.)

God I believe you are my provider, my helper and my healer. I believe you have empowered me to take hold of that which attempts to hold me in bondage. Lord allow me to see and sort through all that is in front of me. Release the spirit of heaviness and brokenness from my life and give me a clean spirit, so that I may approach every issue with a good, positive heart. I declare that I am coming out victorious. Allow me to persevere. It is written, "Blessed is the man who perseveres under trial, because when he has stood the test, he will receive the crown of life that God has promised to those who love him." I believe I have the victory to create a plan and move forward in prayer. I believe you will give me practical steps to resolve my mess so my life can be the masterpiece you intended. Thank you, God. I love you, Father. You are so good to me. My strength is being renewed even now. In Jesus' Name, Amen

And let us not grow weary of doing good, for in due season we will reap, if we do not give up. – Galatians 6:9

But you, take courage! Do not let your hands be weak, for your work shall be rewarded." – 2 Chronicles 15:7

Have I not commanded you? Be strong and courageous. Do not be frightened, and do not be dismayed, for the Lord your God is with you wherever you go. – Joshua 1:9

Do not be slothful in zeal, be fervent in spirit, and serve the Lord. Rejoice in hope, be patient in tribulation, be constant in prayer. – Romans 12:11-12

Come to me, all who labor and are heavy laden, and I will give you rest. – Matthew 11:28

4

A prayer when you need to forgive

> *"For if you forgive others their trespasses, your heavenly Father will also forgive you, but if you do not forgive others their trespasses, neither will your Father forgive your trespasses."*
> *– Matthew 6:14*

SOMEBODY STOLE FROM YOU. SOMEONE HURT YOUR BABY. A family member set you up. A co-worker lied on you. A church member slept with your husband. Your niece was molested by her mother's live in boyfriend. Your neighbor's son bullied your daughter and now she's scarred forever. These are all pretty sad scenarios and all of which happen in real life. Now you may or may not resonate with any of them, but I'm sure you can recall something that happened in your life that was a difficult pill to swallow.

What ever happened, I'm sure it wasn't good and maybe even horrible. It's not fair and it's even challenging to wrap your head around the fact that such things can even happen to the people of God, right? Furthermore, it's even more mind blowing to know that as a believer we are commanded by God to forgive such acts. Whether or not we want to accept it, the truth is, it is written in the Word of God. All of us will have trials as believers. God never promised to isolate us from trials, but He has promised to insulate us, and protect us in the trial! Do I like it? No. But I accept it as law and I trust God's Word and will completely.

I remember watching a talk show about how an older black man and an older white woman became best friends. As teenagers, the white woman wrongly accused the black man of rape and he ended up serving time for most of his adult life. The woman finally felt convicted in her spirit, and came forward to come clean. But it took years before he was released from prison. The talk show host said to the man in the presence of the woman, "how can your families be so connected and how can you be friends with this woman, considering that you lost ten years of your life?" The black man replied, as he held the hand of the white woman, "forgiveness." I had to forgive. That is what the Bible says and I am a believer. It blew me away when I saw it, but I say to you, if you call yourself a believer, then you have to follow God completely. There is no such thing as partial obedience. Partial obedience is disobedience.

Your struggle may be in the area of unforgiveness. As tough as it may be for you to do, forgiveness is a command of God. Not doing so, is only hurting you. Not forgiving your offender is hurting you, draining you, and stressing you out, consuming your life and weighing on your emotions. Not forgiving the one who did it to you will block your blessing and hold up whatever you are believing God for. When you don't forgive, you have no justification. The word says to forgive others as our Father in heaven forgave you (Mathew 6:14.) The Bible doesn't give exceptional circumstances where you are allowed to not forgive someone.

So let me drop this in your spirit, Greatness. You can open up the floodgates of heaven if you simply forgive. For your unforgiveness is blocking your prayer and access to God (Mark 11:25.)

I come to you Judge of All
(Acts 10:42)

Father, in the name of Jesus. I come to you, the only help I know. I come first to say thank you God that you thought enough of me to sacrifice your Son so I would be saved. I thank you for sacrificing your only begotten Son, Jesus so the enemy would not have a claim on me or be able to hold my issues against me. You forgave me before I understood what it meant to be saved. You set me free from sin, and all I can say now is, thank you. I am just grateful to know I belong to you.

But now, God, I come confessing that I have not done as you commanded. I have not been forgiving. I am holding on to stuff. My issues are weighing on me and wearing me down. I need your help Lord and I want you to step in. Strengthen me and guide me. I admit my faith walk may not be where it should be, but I know you love me and your Word says if I confess with a pure heart, I will be forgiven (Romans 10:9) Lord I surrender right here and now. Please, Lord release the hold from my mind, my emotions and my heart. I need to forgive according to your will and your Word. I want to be able to move on with my life. I declare and decree according to the power of the one who holds all power. It is handled in Jesus' name. Amen.

For if you forgive others their trespasses, your heavenly Father will also forgive you, but if you do not forgive others their trespasses, neither will your Father forgive your trespasses. – Matthew 6:14-15

And whenever you stand praying, forgive, if you have anything against anyone, so that your Father also who is in heaven may forgive you your trespasses. – Mark 11:25

If we confess our sins, he is faithful and just to forgive us our sins and to cleanse us from all unrighteousness. – 1 John 1:9

But if you do not forgive others their trespasses, neither will your Father forgive your trespasses. – Matthew 6:15

Then Peter came up and said to him, "Lord, how often will my brother sin against me, and I forgive him? As many as seven times?" Jesus said to him, "I do not say to you seven times, but seventy times seven." – Matthew 18:21-22

5

A prayer when you are struggling to take responsibility

> *"For we are each responsible for our own conduct."*
> **– Galatians 6:5 NLT**

ONE OF THE GREATEST FEELINGS IN THE WORLD FOR ME IS when I stepped up to take personal responsibility for an outstanding debt, apologized for a slight, or course-corrected a situation gone wrong. God has brought me a long way, but I'm not so far removed from my reckless self that I forget the times when I neglected my responsibilities.

In fact, I used to have this recurring theme of not paying parking tickets and then I'd wind up in court having to explain why I had over two dozen parking tickets. It was so irresponsible of me and it was all because I was just lazy. I could make it sound real nice like I was too busy, serving and saving the world or I could use the fall back excuse "I just didn't have time and then I forgot" but there would be no glory in that. Besides God's word says He knows all things and sees all things anyway, so I would only be fooling myself.

On another instance, I borrowed a few hundred dollars from my girlfriend and she couldn't remember me owing her and I couldn't remember paying her back. So years passed, and I didn't think anything of it. We were close. We always vacationed together and we shared space together, but the Holy Spirit nudged me one day, and immediately I stepped up to take responsibility for my actions.

The shift happened only after God began to call me higher and deeper in my faith walk. There was a time when I was really pumping my fist wearing these titles... *Daughter of the King, Child of the Most High* and *Heiress to the Throne*. During that season I remember thinking, "if you are going to wear the title you better make sure you can carry it." In other words, the spirit spoke to me and called me higher. The spirit spoke to my greater self, and the charge was simple and clear: be a woman of integrity. The challenge, however, was to make sure I was walking my talk.

That word was the anchor I needed to take responsibility. Once I knew personal responsibility was a command from God, I had to get it right. It then became a non-negotiable. I didn't want the enemy to use that against me and take me out of the will of God. It had little to do with public humiliation and everything to do with pleasing God. I wanted to be held accountable and held to a higher standard.

Greatness, let me deposit this in your spirit. Personal responsibility is a call higher. When you don't take personal responsibility for your stuff, whatever that stuff may be, you are blocking your blessing. Taking personal responsibility, or the refusal to do so, is one reason so many people struggle in life. You are praying for one thing and believing God for another thing, but on the other hand, you have been irresponsible with other things. This is your chance to fix your life and glorify God in your obedience to His command. It is written: do all things decently and in order (1 Corinthians 14:40.) All things means everything. Make sure you're taking personal responsibility for the mess in your life. It will make you feel better and you can stop hiding and stop running. Whatever you've done that you are not proud of, please resolve to deal with it today. We have all made mistakes and God has forgiven us. But now, it's time for you to take responsibility.

I come to you Everlasting Father
(Isaiah 9:6)

Father, in the name of Jesus, I come to you right now. It is in you that I have my living, my breathing and my being. I confess Jesus the Christ is Lord and I am grateful you sent Your Son to pay the price to cover my sins. Now God I confess I am a sinner saved by grace. I know I didn't earn it and I may not deserve it, but I am eternally grateful for the privilege to be called your daughter. Now God I confess what you already know. So Lord I say move me out of my own way. Reveal to me what I need to know; teach me what you want me to learn and lead me where you want me to go.

Give me clarity about places where I may be standing in my own way. I am learning that I need to take personal responsibility in order step into the woman of integrity that you've called me to be. So help me to be more responsible in personal matters, heart matters, loans, judgment and matters of money and finance. Help me to be more responsible with matters pertaining to my work– my job, my career, my business/ministry. Help me to be more responsible with my relationships – my family, friends, co-workers, colleagues, and acquaintances. Help me to address even the most overwhelming issues and recurring themes in my life like estranged relationships, health issues, misrepresentations, matters of theft and dishonesty. I want to live a long life healthy and well, so please, Lord, would you help me take personal responsibility for my eating, self-care, and all things pertaining to my health. I want to be financially independent. I want to be the first in my family to sow generational wealth into my bloodline so that two or three generations removed will be blessed. I want to own my own business so God please help me to be responsible with all that my employers entrust to me. I want to be loved, appreciated, respected, and admired; so help me to be responsible with every person you bring me in contact with. I only want to sow seeds that will bring me back a beautiful harvest equal or above what I put out.

God, hear my confession and accept my plea. I accept that you are calling me higher in this very moment. I will not allow my irresponsibility to stand in my way. I declare and decree that I will do all things decently and in order according to your Word in 1 Corinthians 14:40. The enemy has no power. It is handled. In Jesus' Name. Amen.

So then each one of us will give an account of himself to God. – Romans 14:12

One who is faithful in a very little is also faithful in much, and one who is dishonest in a very little is also dishonest in much. – Luke 16:10

He who plants and he who waters are one, and each will receive his wages according to his labor. – 1 Corinthians 3:8

But all things should be done decently and in order. – 1 Corinthians 14:40

A slack hand causes poverty, but the hand of the diligent makes rich. – Proverbs 10:4

6

A prayer when you are feeling overwhelmed

> *"Come to me, all who labor and are heavy laden, and I will give you rest."*
> *– Matthew 28:11*

AS MUCH AS SOME PEOPLE BELIEVE I HAVE IT ALL TOGETHER, I don't. *Period.* I work at it every day. If I had it all together I wouldn't have to work at it. And I think that's the big miss. When you are on the outside looking in at other people's lives, you make assumptions based on how they show up in the room. But you don't know or see the tremendous effort they put into it. So yes, there are times when I am overwhelmed by God's blessings chasing me down. However, there are other times when I am extremely overwhelmed by the 'to-do' lists, the number of activities, responsibilities, my demanding schedule and competing priorities, etc. Some days, I am scatter brain, like a chicken with its head cut off. Other days, I am even worse, tipping gently through the day so I don't go into a self-induced meltdown.

There are instances where we unconsciously end up overwhelmed with life... being a mom, wife, daughter, caregiver, business woman, leader and taking care of our personal responsibilities, commitments and such—it can be a lot sometimes. In fact, in most cases, we get so busy being busy that we don't know how we got from point A to point B. We get there because we are simply passengers in life letting life lead us and other people drive us, rather than taking control of our lives. If you are allowing life to lead you, then you are living by default. But if you lead your own life, then you are in the driver's seat, and you are living by design.

Whether you got into this state of being overwhelmed unknowingly or knowingly, the good news is, God can handle it. When I hit a breaking point recently, I reached out to God in the thick of things. I said, "Lord, I don't know where to start today." I mean, I was going to crack if I didn't dial 911 to heaven. It's crazy being in the middle of all kinds of yumminess on one side but so vulnerable and breakable from the load on the other side. I was happy but heavy. I was moving but had to manage it all. I was excited and exhausted at the same darn time. I was getting my money's worth out of life but working overtime in the midst.

If I'm speaking to your spirit right now and you can relate to these breaking points in life from work, home, schedules, to-do lists, relationships, etc. I've got good news for you: God can handle it. If you know what I mean about having the weight of the world on your shoulders, and if you've ever been near a breakdown, I encourage you to seek God right now. He can release you from being overwhelmed if you just let His promises take hold. He promises a perfect plan for your life (Jeremiah 29:11.) He invites you to come to Him when you are weary (Matthew 11:28.) Some things that have become tasks on your list of things to do may not be a part of God's plan to bring you into full alignment with His will. If you draw closer to God and ask Him to reveal His plan, some of your busyness will reveal itself so you can handle it. Then as it pertains to prioritizing your list of things to do, know that God commands us to put Him first in everything. Not only is

God first, but He gives you step-by-step instructions illuminating the path that you should follow next (Psalm 119:105.) Resolving your overwhelmed emotional state is a matter of an ask-and-action. Ask God for release, relief and clarity to sort through the practical matters of your life. Then move into action so that you can see God's hand in your situation.

I come to you God of Order
(1 Corinthians 14:40)

Father, in the name of Jesus, I come to you right now in the truth of where I am. Honestly, I am overwhelmed. My life is wearing me down. I'm tired, exhausted, working very hard and running in all different directions. Some of this is good and some I'm sure is not good for me. I don't have enough time, and I don't know any other way to be.

But God I know you have a plan for my life and your Word says it's a plan to prosper me and to give me hope and a future (Jeremiah 29:11); so I surrender to Your Will for my life. Reveal what you want me to know about the plan and what I am to do and how I can move out of my own way. Teach me and help me to want what you want for my life. I know you created me so there is a greater purpose within me. Now make me ready to receive. Renew my energy. Give me strength were I am weak; breathe fresh wind and air into my being. Give me a restored spirit and the motivation to make adjustments when and where needed. Show me something I've not considered. I'm not attached to my own way, my family's way, or the world's way. I declare and decree as a new creature in Christ that I am committed to putting my life in right order according to Your Word in Matthew 6:33. Lord help me to tune in to you every morning for divine instruction on how to be a better steward of my time. Please move people, places and things off my agenda if they don't line up with what you have for me. I release the spirit of being overwhelmed and give it to you God. I take responsibility for my actions and decisions. I will show up decently and in order from this day forward. It's handled in Jesus' Name.

But Jesus looked at them and said, "With man this is impossible, but with God all things are possible." – Matthew 19:26

For God gave us a spirit not of fear but of power and love and self-control. – 2 Timothy 1:7

Fear not, for I am with you; be not dismayed, for I am your God; I will strengthen you, I will help you, I will uphold you with my righteous right hand. – Isaiah 41:10

Come to me, all who labor and are heavy laden, and I will give you rest. – Matthew 11:28

But he said to me, "My grace is sufficient for you, for my power is made perfect in weakness." Therefore I will boast all the more gladly of my weaknesses, so that the power of Christ may rest upon me. For the sake of Christ, then, I am content with weaknesses, insults, hardships, persecutions, and calamities. For when I am weak, then I am strong. – 2 Corinthians 12:9-10

7
A prayer for order in your life

A T ONE POINT IN MY LIFE, I REMEMBER A MELTDOWN OF tears after digging through three massive garbage bags of mail. I was looking for an important document. This was God's way of revealing just how messy my life was with respect to managing my personal matters. I had no regard for daily responsibility. I didn't like dealing with my mail and I would only pick it up sporadically when I had nothing else to do. I admit, I did not handle small things well like mail or balancing my check book, but I was really good at handling big stuff, like *life* in general, crisis, etc.

This messiness haunted me for a long time and I would openly confess it to be my struggle. I've had numerous occasions and far too many that I would admit to missing important things, dates, bills and even checks as a result of not handling this small but significant personal matter. Years after the meltdown moment, I remember looking throughout the entire house for simple documents that should have been easily accessible. I remember yet again another moment that should have caused me a nervous breakdown. I opened my mail and found a check that was already past the 90 day expiration (INSERT SCREAM HERE)! I wish I could tell you it was just one check that had expired sitting in my neglected mile high mail stuffed in bags waiting to be handled, but it was not. Over a two-year window (maybe three) I remember seeing two or three checks written to me but long expired. I confess, I was a mess until God straightened me out.

If your life is a mess and you have no order; if your life looks picture-perfect on the surface but your back life is just ratchet; if you attempt to take on a task of de-cluttering your life but find that you are back in the same place again; the best hope you have for changing your situation is to know that it is a command of God to do all things decently and in order (1 Corinthians 14:40.)

When you live a messy life, it is not only frustrating, but you are also being disobedient according to the Word. You are getting in your own way of whatever God has for you and you make a bad representation of God. We are all here to represent, or said better, to *re-present* God in the universe, in order to reintroduce the Creator to his creation through our surrender. We are here so that God might make His appeal through us. If you are not at your best, you are not the best vessel for God to work through. When you are not at your best, you are not bringing God glory. If I can be blunt, you are misrepresenting who God is and what He stands for. When you are not at your best, you will not be able to live for and serve God at full capacity. Why? Because you are struggling to get your own life in order. You are called to be an ambassador (2 Corinthians 5:20) and that means representing God by living an orderly life and decent life, which means all things in your physical environment, personhood and external world must line up.

I come to you God my Helper
(Hebrews 13:6)

Father, in the name of Jesus, I come to you admitting that my life is out of order. I love and trust you with my life. I am grateful for this journey and I agree to walk with you. Until now I admit, Lord, that I have not considered bringing this small thing to you. I was preoccupied with other things. But right now, I need you to change, fix and transform this area of my life. Your Word says our reason for living is to glorify you (Isaiah 43:7) and in this moment, I declare I want to be the best representation of you. I want to be better. I want to be the woman you created me to be. You created me better than how I'm living and I now know better. I believe that all Scripture is inspired by you God and is useful to teach me what is true and to make me realize what is wrong in my life. Your Word corrects us when we are wrong and teaches us to do what is right (2 Timothy 3:16.) So I receive this word. I am grateful for this lesson that all things should be done decently and in order (1 Corinthians 14:40.) Help me to put my faith into action. Help me to create a plan to bring order into my life. I commit to taking one single action step today, tomorrow and again on the next day until I get it right. I know I have to do the work as it is written in James 2:17 because faith by itself isn't enough. Unless it produces good deeds, it is dead and useless. I thank you for the nudge in my spirit to get up and take action. Work out my messiness, Lord. Give me the practical tips, practices, and resources to create structure in my life. Help me to manage my life efficiently like a business whereby you give me the policy and procedures. I declare and decree that this small thing has no power. I am able to manage anything and everything in life because Emmanuel is with me. I will manage my living quarters, office, car and daily routines better. I decree that I am a good manager in Jesus' name. I will become an expert in resolving issues and building wealth. I will create an itinerary for my day, week and life. I will handle everything as it comes or in the appropriate time. I can do this because with you, all things are possible. Nothing is too difficult for you. It is handled in Jesus' Name. Amen

And he said to them, "Take care, and be on your guard against all covetousness, for one's life does not consist in the abundance of his possessions." – Luke 12:15

"Do not lay up for yourselves treasures on earth, where moth and rust destroy and where thieves break in and steal, but lay up for yourselves treasures in heaven, where neither moth nor rust destroys and where thieves do not break in and steal. For where your treasure is, there your heart will be also. – Matthew 6:19-21

But all things should be done decently and in order. – 1 Corinthians 14:40

For God is not a God of confusion but of peace. As in all the churches of the saints, – 1 Corinthians 14:33

For kings and all who are in high positions, that we may lead a peaceful and quiet life, godly and dignified in every way. "His master replied, 'Well done, good and faithful servant! You have been faithful with a few things; I will put you in charge of many things. Come and share your master's happiness!' – 1 Timothy 2:2

8

A prayer for disappointing times in your business

IF YOU OWN A BUSINESS, RUN A BUSINESS, STARTING A business or considering closing your business, I'm sure you're no stranger to prayer. The ups and downs of being a business owner are too many to count. In fact you have probably cried over your business several times, if you're anything like me. I'll never forget—just as my business had reached a steady profit growth of over 143%, I got a call from a new client who wanted to pull out of a contract before we even began. The call I was expecting was a call about the start date. But instead, in walks a third party messenger to deliver a well-crafted case to forgo the originally accepted proposal. Needless to say, I was devastated. I had already done the preparation necessary for the project, fore-casted the numbers, counted the win and even allocated some of my earnings to additional expansion initiatives. This contract was going to be the largest project in a single year and certainly a feather in my cap as it pertains to winning larger business contracts. So there I was…shook; but not for long. I considered canceling my vacation plans. I considered pulling back on some things that were already planned. In less than an hour or two, I was already adjusting my sail to accommodate the new winds hitting my boat. I reacted immediately based on the news until I got an attitude adjustment in my spirit.

What I learned in that moment was to put my faith to work in an area of life that typically called for logic, reason, feasibility and business cases. In other words, the best business practices claim that we are to operate based on what we see, not based on what we believe. But faith says we operate on what we believe with no evidence insight. Faith says that we must trust in source and supply which is God our Father, rather than trusting in clients, contracts, deals and buyers, etc. Even with faith, however, there are some things that you have to know as a business owner so that norms are not taken out of context.

There will be ups and downs, good times and bad times, overflow and drought. There will be surprising wins and disappointing losses. You will win if you put in the work, but sometimes you will lose even though you have done nothing wrong. The painful losses may have to do with how you show up or how you run your business and whether or not you are the best person for the opportunity. Either way, we have to be prepared for times when it will just be a loss. This has nothing to do with how you show up, or how you perform, or how you do business. It's the nature of the beast. Sometimes it will make sense and other times it won't. But how you move through those disappointing losses will give you the rite of passage into business ownership.

After having a few hours to digest the disappointing phone call, I shifted my attitude and something in me began to speak up. I heard myself saying, "God, I trust you. I'm not going to accept this as a loss because I trust that you are my source. I trust, God that you have given me this opportunity and you are able to give me over and above it. I will not allow the enemy to convince me that all is lost. I trust that you are working and moving on my behalf right now. I trust you for exceedingly and abundantly above that contract. I believe you have something greater for me right now God." Do you see how I shifted my energy? Can you see how I began to line up my behavior with my faith so that I could stand congruent with what I said I believed? I took this as a testing of my faith. God really wants to see our behavior line up with our faith. I believe God wanted to see how much of my reliance was in that contract versus how much of my dependency was on Him. Within 24 hours, I was miles away at a business networking conference and I literally sat discussing a 1 billion dollar project with one of the most powerful businessmen ever. He offered, in that meeting, to support my business all because I trusted God and I didn't get stuck looking at a resource.

So let me drop this in your spirit. Never allow one setback or one loss or one defeat or one disappointing moment or one "no sale" or one canceled project, to steal your steam, minimize your light or cause you to give up on what is in your belly. The enemy comes to steal, kill and destroy your spirit. He comes to disrupt your idea and derail your business by planting seeds of doubt as it relates to your ability to create wealth. However, if you resist when you get that disappointing call and shift into praise, God will deliver. The Word says, "It is God who gives you the ability to create wealth." If God gives you the ability, then certainly He will make room for your gift. He will assign those who need what you have to offer and He will assign consumers and clients to you if you believe and call it forth. If you can draw a clear line of distinction that your business is not just a good idea but God's instruction, then trust and believe that nothing will be lost despite what it looks like. Just keep pressing.

I come to you Jehovah-Nissi, The Lord My Banner
(Exodus 17:15)

Father, in the name of Jesus, I come to you to thank you for allowing me the privilege and the opportunity to step out in the business you placed in my heart, mind and spirit. God I am nothing without you. You created me and your eyes saw my unformed body when I was made in a secret place according to Psalms 139. So, I know that it is you who gives me the ability to create wealth. I know that I am not my own and it is You, Lord who created me to do good work that You prepared in advance for me to do according to Your Word in Ephesians 2:10. Lord, I believe Your Word "if you faithfully obey the voice of the Lord your God being careful to do all these commandments that I command you today, the Lord your God will set you high above all the nations of the earth. And all these blessings shall come upon you and overtake you if you obey the voice of the Lord your God" (Deuteronomy 28:1-3.) It is written "The Lord will make your businesses and your farms successful." I trust you Lord to do it in any way you choose. Help me to be open and accepting of your will and not my will. It is written, "The Lord will make you successful in your daily work." God, I trust you to order my steps day by day and to give me divine instructions in my "to do" list on my priorities, objectives and goals. In particular, grant me favor with those whom I do business. Let all of this be your will, your way and if it is not your will, please redirect me to the way that you know best. I declare and decree that I am successful in everything I do. My harvest will be so large that my storehouses will be full according to Deuteronomy 28. Now Lord help me to resist the enemy's attempts to discourage me through normal business. Build up my confidence in you so I will not flinch. Give me courage, knowledge, wisdom, fresh ideas and the ability to do what I need to do and then hire, partner, retain resources and services to fill the necessary gaps. Lord, give me the discipline to meditate on the word day and night so that I may be able to do all that is written in your word. As you made Joshua a recipient of abundance, I declare and decree I will be prosperous and have good success according to your word in Joshua 1:8.

This Book of the Law shall not depart from your mouth, but you shall meditate on it day and night, so that you may be careful to do according to all that is written in it. For then you will make your way prosperous, and then you will have good success. – Joshua 1:8

And God is able to make all grace abound to you, so that having all sufficiency in all things at all times, you may abound in every good work. – 2 Corinthians 9:8

Not that I am speaking of being in need, for I have learned in whatever situation I am to be content. I know how to be brought low, and I know how to abound. In any and every circumstance, I have learned the secret of facing plenty and hunger, abundance and need. – Philippians 4:11-12

And if you faithfully obey the voice of the Lord your God, being careful to do all his commandments that I command you today, the Lord your God will set you high above all the nations of the earth. And all these blessings shall come upon you and overtake you, if you obey the voice of the Lord your God. Blessed shall you be in the city, and blessed shall you be in the field. Blessed shall be the fruit of your womb and the fruit of your ground and the fruit of your cattle, the increase of your herds and the young of your flock. Blessed shall be your basket and your kneading bowl. – Deuteronomy 28:1-68

And let us not grow weary of doing good, for in due season we will reap, if we do not give up. – Galatians 6:9

But remember the LORD your God, for it is he who gives you the ability to produce wealth, and so confirms his covenant, which he swore to your ancestors, as it is today. – Deuteronomy 8:18

9

A prayer for overcoming insecurity

> *"You are altogether beautiful, my love;*
> *there is no flaw in you."*
> **– Song of Solomon 4:7**

INSECURITY MAY SEEM LIKE SOMETHING THAT DOES NOT require much tending to, but if you do not work at resolving it, it will continue to show up in your life. It will disrupt your emotional wellbeing and alter your perspective about everything. One of the biggest lessons I had in my life about insecurity showed up in my twenties. I was a young woman at the time, and I had this consistent issue of overcompensating. I didn't know it at the time, but life and time will show you who you are if you take good notes. In fact, I remember very distinctly when God nudged me the first time. It was a defining moment when a woman passerby in church complimented me on my look, my outfit, my shoes, my hair and my overall package. It was a well-intended compliment that didn't sit well with me but it was just God trying to get my attention.

The compliment didn't land well because there was a disturbance in my spirit. I reckoned (yes reckoned) this is God. In that defining moment, God revealed to me that he was calling me higher. Part of that moment came with an awareness that I was out of balance like a see saw. The compliment about my outer appearance called out into question "aren't I more than just all things fabulous on the outside?" So there was a conflict, to which I'm sure you can relate, when your self-perception and others external perception of you don't line up. I learned while others were seeing just my external self, I believed my real self, my heart, my walk, my love for God was more visible but it was not. Out of that came an "aha" moment: I was focusing more attention on my outer than on my inner self and it was an overcompensation to cover up my insecurity, which I later discovered was attached to me not finishing college immediately after high school. That was my experience. But it led me to asking God the right sequence of questions that resulted in a journey to sure up my identity, self-worth, mission and purpose.

Now I didn't have major falls as a result of my insecurity because early on I got my "come to Jesus" call. However, because I work with so many women now I see signs of insecurity showing up in many ways that are much more painful than they have to be. I think the major areas are: not knowing who you are, whose you are, and not knowing your uniqueness and value. I've seen women show up very controlling or stalker-like in relationships worried about what their significant other is doing. That's a sign of insecurity. Another sign is women show up very sensitive, thin skinned and they tend to take everything personal. That's a sign of insecurity. Another situation is when you don't ask for what you want and step out on what's in your heart. That's also a sign of insecurity.

20 Signs of Insecurity:

1. sensitive to other people's comments
2. easily offended
3. comparing yourself to other people
4. withdrawing when in the presence of others

5. overcompensating with material things
6. over-identifying with a job, title, position or role
7. sensitive to the misspelling of your name or needing your name to be announced
8. necessary inclusion of title and/or credentials in public
9. the need to be identified or classified
10. holding others well above yourself
11. need to make a case for who you are and what you know
12. inability to speak up for yourself
13. inability to ask for what you want
14. fear of the unknown
15. judgment and criticism of others
16. always putting others first
17. apologizing for things that aren't your responsibility
18. making a request or demand in the form of a question
19. taking everything personally
20. controlling behavior to monitor relationships

The best way to resolve insecurity is to acknowledge it, pray about it and then move into action to resolve it. You resolve it best in self-discovery. The reason you show up the way that you do is because you are struggling with comparing yourself to others. Or, perhaps you do not feel worthy because you lack self-knowledge. Regardless of the root of your insecurity, the sweet thing is you are not alone. It's no surprise that you struggle in this area because like most of us, we've never had a course on self-awareness, self-discovery or self-acceptance. We were brought into a world where success was recognized by status and credentials. These are shallow and surface benchmarks that see you not by your uniqueness, but judge you by your scores, ranks, and corporate levels of achievement, etc. So, forgive yourself right now for not knowing what you didn't know before you knew it. Work at finding your unique gift and purpose in the world. Consider a personal identify or gift inventory on your journey, invest in your growth and development or try to increase your social learning time and decrease your intake of entertainment.

I come to you Elohim the strong one
(Psalm 19:1)

Father, God in the name of Jesus, I come to lay my issues with insecurity and my questions of self-worth at your feet. I don't know who I am at times, and I tend to question my value altogether. I consistently feel overwhelmed in my thinking about what others have versus what I have. In the presence of others, I find myself drawing back and feeling uncomfortable. Lord, thinking about what I don't have, (things like education/house/car/job/money/husband) makes me less than. But I turn the corner today, God, for I am encouraged. Forgive me for being blind to your wonderful works that created me in your image. Forgive me for being critical of myself and for judging every imperfection. I now know that my self-criticism is a jab at you because I am your masterpiece. Forgive me for not appreciating how you made me. Forgive me for having little faith in the plan and purpose you have for me.

I declare and decree, you are my God; so I now step into seeing myself as you see me. Lord, I accept that I am here on purpose and for a purpose. It is written, "In him we have obtained an inheritance, having been predestined according to the purpose of him who works all things according to the counsel of his will." (Ephesians 1:10.) Lord, I accept that I was created in your image fearfully and wonderfully made according to your Word in Psalms 139:15. Lord I declare and decree I am nothing without you but I am all-sufficient with you, because of you. Help me to transform my mind; to take off my old self and my old way of thinking and to put on my new self so I can think like you. Lord, destroy every negative word spoken over my life. Delete every label that does not meet your definition of me in Your Word. Cancel the damaging effects of years of abuse/hate/ worthless talk. I believe nothing is too hard for you and all things are possible with you. Have your way and let your perfect will be done, in Jesus' Name. Amen.

So God created man in his own image, in the image of God he created him; male and female he created them. – Genesis 1:27

Before I formed you in the womb I knew you, and before you were born I consecrated you; I appointed you a prophet to the nations. – Jeremiah 1:5

For am I now seeking the approval of man, or of God? Or am I trying to please man? If I were still trying to please man, I would not be a servant of Christ. – Galatians 1:10

But let each one test his own work, and then his reason to boast will be in himself alone and not in his neighbor. – Galatians 6:4

Not that we are sufficient in ourselves to claim anything as coming from us, but our sufficiency is from God, – 2 Corinthians 3:5

10
A prayer for resolution of money issues...

"In the same way, faith by itself, if it is not accompanied by action, is dead."

– James 2:17

RUST ME, I BELIEVE GOD WANTS US TO BRING EVERYTHING before Him. I believe the Word that God promises to supply our every need. I believe He will give us the desires of our heart. However I believe there is a big miss about these truths and our prayer to God about our financial matters. We pray about money issues and expect financial breakthroughs to show up in the form of random checks in the mail. The truth of the matter is "Surprise money" will not resolve your issue of not having enough. And I'm certainly not judging because there was a time in my life that I'm sure I prayed for more miracle money. I somehow believed that God would miraculously move on my behalf to resolve every dollar that I needed to get me out of the mess I created. Because honestly, that's what it would've been. Very often, we make poor financial decisions with our money and expect God to get us out of the hole we dug. We buy what we want and we beg for what we need. Or we spend money we don't have and we live above our means. If you're reading this far, I'm sure you can relate.

But would you allow me to drop this in your spirit, my sister friend? Release yourself from the shame and guilt of mismanaging your money. Forgive yourself for not knowing how to manage your money. Forgive yourself for just being irresponsible. Forgive yourself for having expensive taste that you cannot *YET* afford. Stop beating yourself up about your struggle with money. Stop blaming other people and your creditors. Stop questioning whether God hears you. Stop wearing yourself down in your prayers and decide right now that you're going to make a change.

To fix your money situation, here is the most important thing that you must know. You don't need God to miraculously fix what He has already empowered you to do. You certainly should seek His guidance in all things, however you don't need to delegate to God. God is not Santa Claus or the lottery. He is our Father and He expects better from us. God has equipped you to do better and to have more. There are some things in life that we need God's divine hand to move (things like terminal illness, mental illness, water drought, natural disaster and other things where there is no man-made solution.) But as far as our money situation goes, God wired us in such a way that we have the ability to work through our money issues. There is no lack of money in the universe so we shouldn't pray to God for more; it's already there. We should pray however for God to forgive us for not being a good steward. Then, we should ask God to help us with additional revenue streams, responsible management, and the discipline to tithe. Understand this: "faith without works is dead." This is an area that requires you to pray, plan, and then work your plan. This is an area where you will be required to do the work. Transition from delegating your prayers to God as you stand in hope for God to send a miracle. Begin to pray for wisdom and discipline so that God can help you to make better decisions regarding your money.

This is doable, but it's going to take time. If you continue to do the same things, then you're going to get the same results. If you want something you've never had, then you must do something that you've never done.

I come to you Jehovah-Jireh the one who provides
(Genesis 22:13-14)

Father God, in the name of Jesus, I come to you right now for your guidance. Please teach me in the area, guide me and enable me to change my mind set and begin to reconcile my money issues so I can make more responsible financial decisions. Lord, I lay this down before you. There is a deficit in my purse, bank account, emergency fund, retirement fund, God, and I need your direction on how to generate more. Lord, forgive me for not being a responsible steward of my resources. Forgive me for not being faithful with my tithing. Honestly, I have been out of order with regard to money management. It is written "But everything should be done in a fitting and orderly way" so Lord I lay before you my desire to better manage my resources. Today I will speak those things as though they are right now until they are. I am speaking in faith in agreement with what I know is possible with you. So I declare and decree that I am a better steward over my money today. I declare and decree that I have more than enough. I declare and decree that I am a tither and a giver, not a taker or a cheater. I declare and decree that I am paid my worth. I declare and decree that all my debts are paid, my credit score is above average; I am now a lender and not a borrower; my name is great and God has made me a distributor, an investor and philanthropist. Now, Lord, help me to put pen to paper in order to create a plan. Point me to the right resources and experts, and send an accountability partner to me for moments when I am weary. In Jesus' name, I trust that it is done, Amen.

The rich rules over the poor, and the borrower is the slave of the lender. – Proverbs 22:7

Therefore do not be anxious, saying, 'What shall we eat?' or 'What shall we drink?' or 'What shall we wear?' For the Gentiles seek after all these things, and your heavenly Father knows that you need them all. But seek first the kingdom of God and his righteousness, and all these things will be added to you. – Matthew 6:31-33

A good man leaves an inheritance to his children's children, but the sinner's wealth is laid up for the righteous. – Proverbs 13:22

If then you have not been faithful in the unrighteous wealth, who will entrust to you the true riches? – Luke 16:11

Wealth gained hastily will dwindle, but whoever gathers little by little will increase it. – Proverbs 13:11

11

A prayer for a heartbreaking-gut punch

"Blessed is the man who remains steadfast under trial, for when he has stood the test he will receive the crown of life, which God has promised to those who love him."
– James 1:12

EVER GET A CALL THAT FEELS LIKE SOMEBODY JUST PUNCHED you in the stomach? You know the call that comes in the middle of the night or in the early morning at an odd hour that makes your heart race. *You know the call.* It comes from a family member or a close friend that makes you tense up. It is the call delivering bad news. *Auntie was found not breathing. God Mom was diagnosed with cancer.* Brother was in a car crash. Cousin is missing. Uncle was just arrested. Nephew is in psych ward. Sister just revealed uncle molested her. Brother just pressed charges on son beating mother. This would be a gut punch. It knocks the wind right out of you. It is the reason we fall to our knees immediately as we should.

No one wants the gut punch but the truth is if you keep on living chances are you will get knocked down. The good news is if you play your position right you will be able to get back up and if you master this lesson over time you will be able to stand firm and hold your ground. I've learned to hold my ground early on when the call came that my brother was killed in a car crash. I held it together and had a delayed meltdown months later. I've had other instances where I've held it together and took deep breaths. Eventually with more occasions I learned how to deal and was able to stand firmly and take it. The way you take the hit and pass on the option to have a meltdown is to immediately call on Jesus, breathe deep, settle yourself and go back to God ask Him to completely take over...take over and control your mind, emotions, reaction, actions and response.

Let me encourage you. Maybe you are going through as a result of a gut punch. Maybe you have been suffering for some time. We often suffer unnecessarily when we don't go to the Lord, our Comforter. We often suffer unnecessarily because we have not disciplined ourselves in good time to know how to handle crisis in bad times. We often suffer or delay the opportunity to have peace in our storm when we don't go to God. We are so caught in the shock and hurt of the punch we just can't bring ourselves to pray. God will honor your prayer and He will honor your cries for help if you just turn to Him. God will honor your request for divine intervention but you must believe and ask. Once you reach out to God, you will have an increase in strength, discernment, wisdom, clarity and peace of mind. When you are solid then you will be able to stand in the gap for your family.

If you've never had a gut punch, just keep on living. My word of advice for you is to build yourself up in prayer beforehand. Proactively pray against the storms that will come to shake your very foundation.

I come to you Author of Peace
(1 Corinthians 14:33)

Father, in the name of Jesus, I come to you right now Lord in a moment of despair. I come to you to place this [name it] in your hands. I am [shocked /devastated /hurt /confused / overwhelmed /sad /angry]. My heart is heavy but I know that you are a heart fixer. Your Word says in Matthew 11:28, "Come to me, all you who are weary and burdened, and I will give you rest." I am here, Lord standing on Your Word. Lord, I know that you are not absent but you are here. I thank You, Lord for forewarning me through Your Word. I accept that in life there will be tribulation. So I thank You, Lord that even though I desire isolation -to be kept from any trial, struggle, hurt or harm, You are the insulation that protects me through it. Lord I know that you are with me and I am grateful. Stay with me my heart is broken, bruised and my spirit is crushed. I ask because it is written "The Lord is near to the brokenhearted and saves the crushed in spirit." (Psalm 34:18) Have your way. Hold us up. I trust you to be present. I trust you to comfort. I trust you to lead, guide and direct. I trust you for divine turn around/resolution/healing and mercy. I declare it done. In Jesus' name. Amen.

I have said these things to you, that in me you may have peace. In the world you will have tribulation. But take heart; I have overcome the world. – John 16:33

The Lord is near to the brokenhearted and saves the crushed in spirit. – Psalm 34:18

More than that, we rejoice in our sufferings, knowing that suffering produces endurance, and endurance produces character, and character produces hope, and hope does not put us to shame, because God's love has been poured into our hearts through the Holy Spirit who has been given to us. – Romans 5:3-5

Beloved, do not be surprised at the fiery trial when it comes upon you to test you, as though something strange were happening to you. But rejoice insofar as you share Christ's sufferings, that you may also rejoice and be glad when his glory is revealed.
– 1 Peter 4:12-13

Blessed is the man who remains steadfast under trial, for when he has stood the test he will receive the crown of life, which God has promised to those who love him.
– James 1:12

12

A prayer when you are struggling with discipline

> *"For this very reason, make every effort to supplement your faith with virtue, and virtue with knowledge, and knowledge with self-control, and self-control with steadfastness, and steadfastness with godliness, and godliness with brotherly affection, and brotherly affection with love."*
> **– 2 Peter 1:5-7**

ONE OF THE THINGS I'VE STRUGGLED WITH OVER THE course of my life is discipline. It's interesting that my struggle however is not that I am not disciplined at all; it's just that in some areas, I am really good and in other areas, I am not so good. As of late, I can really say I now get it. I know how to discipline myself when I have something in front of me that is really meaningful to me, but it's taken me years to master. So now, because I am afforded the opportunity to work with women around the world I, can see and confirm that I am not alone. Many of us struggle with discipline (or the lack thereof.)

Here's what we have to know. You must know that in order to get from where you are to where you want to be, it's going to require discipline to get you there. Discipline is a necessary friend that helps us to get to our ideal self and our ideal life. Think about an athlete who is focused on the game and the sport. They clearly have an end goal, which is to win. They also have a strategy in order to plan out how they will win. Part of their strategy for winning and part of that same strategy to move them from average to exceptional requires discipline. An athlete must eat, sleep and breathe the sport. He or she must get up every day, no matter how they feel to do the necessary work in order to reach the end goal. Likewise, as a woman of faith, consider discipline to be your friend. It is the vehicle that is going to transport you from where you are to where you want to be. If you are trying to figure out why you can't go to bed at a certain hour or why you can't write your book on a consistent basis, maybe it has to do with discipline. If you're struggling to figure out why you can't exercise on a regular schedule or why you can't push back from the table or why you can't take an hour for yourself every day, I guarantee you: all of that has to do with discipline. Discipline is doing what you have to do now so you can do what you want to do later. When you have discipline you are doing the hard work without being told, embracing delayed gratification, and you are constantly training new muscles that are underdeveloped. However, if you train the muscle of discipline, it will be strengthened. How we get to a point of establishing the muscle of discipline is to know and believe it's possible.

The Word of the Lord says, "I have given you a sound mind and self control." Because we have self-control, you must accept that God wired you in such a way that you have the ability to control your actions and behaviors. Be aware of the areas where you need discipline. Train like an athlete every day, and do the work. Avoid beating yourself up. Discipline doesn't happen overnight. So take your time, and work at it every day. As you do, celebrate your small wins.

I come to you Lamb of God
(John 1:29)

Father, in the name of Jesus, I come to you in complete surrender to your will and your way for my life. Lord until now I'm not sure I understood your instructions. Lord forgive me for not knowing and heeding your word about how I am to show up as a daughter of the King. Now I reject my old way of being inconsistent and claiming I have no discipline. God I accept you are calling me higher. I accept your standard for my life to do all things decent and in order. I admit I am challenged when it comes to doing what I need to do. Lord release me from being controlled by my feelings and emotions. Lord help me to develop discipline in all areas of my life including very practical matters. Lord help me to develop and maintain discipline even in areas that are holding me back from being the best representation of you. I want to be your Ambassador so won't you please move me out of my own way. Enable me to show up to me to be self-controlled as your word says. I thank you now for moving on behalf to transform me. I believe I can do it Lord according to your power at work in me. Your word says it and I believe it … that the Fruit of the Spirit is self-control and it resides in me. I declare it done right now Lord. I declare and decree I shall move in the direction you lead me to go to do the necessary work to break the chains that hold me down. In Jesus' Name. Amen

A man without self-control is like a city broken into and left without walls. – Proverbs 25:28

No temptation has overtaken you that is not common to man. God is faithful, and he will not let you be tempted beyond your ability, but with the temptation he will also provide the way of escape, that you may be able to endure it. – 1 Corinthians 10:13

But the fruit of the Spirit is love, joy, peace, patience, kindness, goodness, faithfulness, gentleness, self-control; against such things there is no law. – Galatians 5:22-23

For this very reason, make every effort to supplement your faith with virtue, and virtue with knowledge, and knowledge with self-control, and self-control with steadfastness, and steadfastness with godliness, and godliness with brotherly affection, and brotherly affection with love. – 2 Peter 1:5-7

But I discipline my body and keep it under control, lest after preaching to others I myself should be disqualified. – 1 Corinthians 9:24-27

13

A prayer for a life makeover

"For I know the plans I have for you," declares the LORD,
*"plans to prosper you and not to harm you, plans to give
you hope and a future."*
– Jeremiah 29:11 NIV

I F YOU THINK ABOUT IT, IT WOULD BE PRETTY DISRESPECTFUL to pray to God for a new life. I mean, there was a time when I embraced the concept of making over your life, reinventing yourself, and changing your life. However, it just occurred to me how much of an insult that would be to God to say "I don't really want this life that you gave me. Instead, I want a new one!" Lord forgive us for not knowing what didn't know before we knew better. So if you are feeling like you REALLY do need a life makeover, or if you want a do-over in life, let me help you resolve this.

It is perfectly fine that you desire to be in a different place right now, which may have a lot to do with you going through a tough season. Maybe you just came out of a difficult relationship. Maybe you lost a love one. Maybe you lost a job, or you had an unfortunate circumstance happen to you that resulted in a domino effect in other areas of your life. Maybe your bank account is in the red, or your credit score is below zero and your debt is beyond reconciliation. Whatever it is that leaves you feeling like you're living in a real-life nightmare, consider this before you run away from the life God has blessed you with. You are a believer and therefore you belong to God. God created you and He knows all about your situation. He holds a plan in his hand for your life and that plan is to prosper you. In fact, the Word of the Lord in Jeremiah 29:11 says, "God's plan is to give you hope and a future." The word hope is your light at the end of the tunnel. If you didn't have God or know God you would not have the promise of hope and the knowing that there's a plan in play. The hallmark of a believer is that we have hope. That means, whatever your situation is right now, God has given you a promise to bring you into a better place to prosper you. Because God has a plan for your life, you have to believe that He knows your current situation. Therefore, it is likely that He is doing something far beyond your comprehension. Everything is purposeful. Nothing in your life will be wasted. For the Word of the Lord says there will be trials and tribulation but God will bring us through all of it. James 2:2-4 "My brothers and sisters, when you have many kinds of troubles, you should be full of joy, because you know that these troubles test your faith, and this will give you patience. Let your patience show itself perfectly in what you do. Then you will be perfect and complete and will have everything you need."

Trust that God is working *in* you and *on* you so He can work *through* you. Whatever you went through, you are coming out of it! God is going to restore you. You will be better at the end of this. God is working His craft to stretch you, grow you and increase your capacity for more. God is evolving you into the person He created you to be. The situation and circumstance that you are going through is purposeful. Rather than asking God for a new life, ask God for the life He has for you and to keep you while you are a work in progress.

I come to you Author of my Faith
(Hebrews 12:2)

Father, in the name of Jesus, I come to you Lord thanking you God for life and eternal life. Forgive me, Lord, for being ungrateful for the air I breathe every day. I confess that you are my Lord and Savior and I believe and receive according to your Word that your eyes saw my unformed body when I was made in the secret place; so I declare I am yours. I confess it is in you that I have my living, my breathing and my being. I believe your Word in Jeremiah 29 that you have a perfect plan for my life. Now God, bring me through this unbearable situation. Allow me to get the lesson and increase my capacity for whatever you have for me. Move me out of my own way. Show me what I need to work on. Reveal to me where I am to surrender to your perfect will. Give me strength, patience, endurance and the ability to surrender. I don't want a new life God; more exactly, I want the life *you* have for me. I declare it is done in Jesus' name, Amen.

My brothers and sisters, when you have many kinds of troubles, you should be full of joy, 3 because you know that these troubles test your faith, and this will give you patience. 4 Let your patience show itself perfectly in what you do. Then you will be perfect and complete and will have everything you need. – James 2:2

Behold, I am doing a new thing; now it springs forth, do you not perceive it? I will make a way in the wilderness and rivers in the desert. – Isaiah 43:19

Your eyes saw my unformed body; all the days ordained for me were written in your book before one of them came to be – Psalm 139:16 NIV

For I know the plans I have for you," declares the LORD, "plans to prosper you and not to harm you, plans to give you hope and a future – Jeremiah 29:11 NIV

For we are God's handiwork, created in Christ Jesus to do good works, which God prepared in advance for us to do. – Ephesians 2:10 NIV

14
A prayer for good friends

"Two are better than one, because they have a good reward for their toil. For if they fall, one will lift up his fellow. But woe to him who is alone when he falls and has not another to lift him up! Again, if two lie together, they keep warm, but how can one keep warm alone? And though a man might prevail against one who is alone, two will withstand him—a threefold cord is not quickly broken."
– Ecclesiastes 4:9-12

O NE DAY, WHILE DRIVING BACK TO NEW JERSEY FROM Washington DC, my girlfriend Marilyn and I were chatting it up about technology. Our three dogs (Sophie, Jordan and Barkley) were squeezed into this tiny little "designer car" and we drove along the busy thruway, looking at Apple apps. If you heard the conversation, you would've thought she had just given me $1 million when she pointed me to one particular app. My response was, "you just earned this friendship and I'm going to keep you." We both fell out laughing. I said, "See, this is what I'm talking about. You brought value to this relationship, my friend, and you always do it with these tiny deposits!" We laughed and embellished the idea of earning friendships by making tiny deposits.

But since then, I joke around with my other girlfriends every now and again. I'll say something crazy like, "you know what ... I appreciate you for this breath mint you just handed me. You just earned a few more years." My girlfriend Rhonda will get into a laughing fit at how hysterical it is to qualify. But it really is my light hearted way of loving and appreciating friendships for the value they bring into my life. On the flip side, I remember once giving my buddy Rhonda an idea for a project she was working on for her kids. She thought it was brilliant and got a little emotional. I said to her, "I know ....I earned my friendship. Rhonda you will have to keep me as a friend because who would come up with all these brilliant ideas and make you laugh and cry." Michellene, another one of my good friends, is such a wonderful person. I have stalled just to share my gratitude for the friendship because it really is divine. I've said on a number of occasions "there are no words to adequately describe my appreciation" and she'll respond in kind "ditto." The moral of the story is to be a good friend to others and you will attract quality friends to yourself. I have the best group of friends who are just plain ole good, yummy, and fabulous people.

If you don't have friends, or if you realize that you need to change your circle, guess what, Greatness? You don't need permission to do it. Just do it. In fact, if your friend circle scenario is quite opposite of the yummy girl power friends I mentioned, and if you find yourself in a group with people who are negative, jealous, evil, and mean, then change friends now. If your circle of friends lack goals, ambition, or drive, and most of the time, they are takers and back stabbers, you've got to change things up. Let me encourage you to act now. You can't choose your family, but you can choose your friends. You can absolutely choose who you associate with even if you are forced into spaces with people who don't share your way of thinking. It's fair and reasonable to think that there will come a day when you will need your girlfriend to offer you a word of encouragement. There will come a day when you will want to have girl talk over brunch or a day at the spa. There will come a day when you dream and plan a fantastic idea, but you will need that extra boost of confidence. There will come a day when you get a devastating blow and you will need a friend to come pick you up off the floor. There will come a day when you need someone to pray you through the other side of your situation. You have every right to long for a good friend and to get what you want.

How do you attract quality, awesome, amazing people into your life? Be a quality person. Be awesome yourself. Be amazing yourself! You don't attract what you want or what you need; you attract who you are! So if you become better as a person, then you will attract better people. Have a standard for yourself and then you will have a standard for the kinds of people with whom you associate. For instance, I just don't associate with mean and evil people. We cannot be friends if you are nice to me but you are mean to other people. I don't particularly care for stingy people. You cannot be nice to me and then refuse to tip when we're out to dinner. You can't be a complainer and be friends with me. I don't entertain regular telephone calls with people who complain. These are just some of my standards. In the same way, you must have some standards for yourself. When you do, you will attract back people with similar standards. Then it will be easier to discern where you have a genuine connection with people. Be intentional about who you want in your life. When you meet really good people, it's okay to find a way to stay in touch without being aggressive or needy. Allow the relationship to unfold organically. Trust your instinct to know where to place people in your life. In other words, everyone doesn't deserve a front row seat in your life. You are the sum total of the top five people whom you spend time with. So be careful who you spend your time with.

I come to you El-Elyon the most high God
(Genesis 14:17)

Father, in the name of Jesus, I come to you to lay before you my desire to be a better friend. Lord God I desire to be the friend who sticks closer than a brother, and I desire to have good girl-friends who will stick by me through thick and thin. Lord I desire to be able to have friends who will pick up the phone and be there when I need them. I resist every attempt of the enemy to move closer to me through the people around me. Lord, remove those people from my life. Distance me, oh Lord, from those who are negative, jealous, mean and evil. Allow them to just fall away so that I can love them from afar. I believe, oh God, in peaceful transitions of distance from people who don't love me or support me. I believe, oh God, and receive that there is often a pruning process that has to happen on my behalf. Forgive me, God, for not being the best friend that I could be. Make me better, God. Make me a better woman according to your Word. Allow me to be a role model for others and an ambassador for you to re-present you in the earth in the name of good friendships. Bring me closer to women of God who are about their father's business. I believe your Word says iron sharpens iron and so I welcome the opportunity to be sharpened. It is in Jesus' name that I leave these prayers at your feet. In Jesus' name, Amen.

A man of many companions may come to ruin, but there is a friend who sticks closer than a brother. – Proverbs 18:24

Two are better than one, because they have a good reward for their toil. For if they fall, one will lift up his fellow. But woe to him who is alone when he falls and has not another to lift him up! Again, if two lie together, they keep warm, but how can one keep warm alone? And though a man might prevail against one who is alone, two will withstand him—a threefold cord is not quickly broken. – Ecclesiastes 4:9-12

Iron sharpens iron, and one man sharpens another. – Proverbs 27:17

Therefore, encourage one another and build one another up, just as you are doing. – 1 Thessalonians 5:11

Do not be deceived: "Bad company ruins good morals." – 1 Corinthians 15:33

15
A prayer for more time

> "So then, each of us will give an
> account of ourselves to God."
> – **Romans 14:12**

I HAVE BEEN TIME CHALLENGED FOR A LONG TIME. MY MOTHER stepped in one season and really educated me on the beauty of being on time and it helped eventually. However my very first real lesson on time management was years prior. When I was a young professional working on Wall Street, there was a mandatory training session everybody had to participate in called Franklin Covey. I'll never forget when it was my day to attend the training I adamantly asked that I be allowed to skip the session because I didn't have time to learn about time management. Thankfully I wasn't able to get out of the class because that workshop changed my life. I learned that time management was not about time management at all. It was about being congruent with what you say you believe and value and how you must line up your behavior to support that. That session taught me about purpose and life mission but years later I still struggled with time.

It wasn't until years later I received one of the best lessons I ever learned on the subject of time which came from my mentor,

Dr. Barbara Skinner Williams. It was interesting how the topic of time came up through a graduate level leadership program as one of the critical success factors for today's leaders. Her lesson was "you don't own time, God owns time." In other words, time is not yours to waste. Those words shook me to the core. Perhaps it was the idea that I would be held accountable for how I manage the time God entrusted to me. After years of struggling with this it was her words that led to my course correction on being more responsible with time. In the same season I learned another success tip around time from The Honorable Alexis Herman who shared her wisdom on how to manage it all, she said, "You have to schedule everything and put yourself on your calendar." Even before hearing from Dr. Skinner and The Honorable Alexis Herman, my other mentor Pastor and former boss Dr. Soaries once taught a lesson about how to manage time and priorities using the NCAA Sweet 16 bracket formula. So the trend was that all of these successful people share this quality high-value life skill: time management.

My point is this, woman of God: time is one of your most valuable commodities because you cannot get it back. God gives us our time in daily disbursements. He gives us 86,400 units of time and when He wakes you up and places 24 hours in our hand, it's like sand quickly moving through your fingers. Once it's gone you can never get it back. If you wasted it, there's no recovering it. When you mismanage time, you are out of order because you don't own it. It was that lesson alone that helped me to understand my responsibility with time and how God will hold each of us accountable for how we spend it. You own nothing. God owns everything. And He requires that you manage what He has placed in your hand. How you manage time is to understand time and know where time goes. Whatever you choose to do with time, understand that it falls in one of three buckets. It is either an investment, a cost, or a waste. An investment will advance you, costs will withdraw from you, and wasted time will rob you of your fullness and abundance. When you allow distractions to steal your time the enemy goes to work stealing your time, and working to destroy every chance and opportunity you get to become who God created you to be.

I come to you El-Shaddai
Lord God Almighty
(Psalm 91:1)

Father, in the name of Jesus, I come before you to thank you for life today. I thank you for time and I ask your forgiveness for moments when I have mismanaged my time. I confess, Lord, that you are the owner of time and the keeper of time. I receive that time you give me is only mine to manage. Help me to honor time and respect other people's time as well. Help me to discern when the enemy is distracting me from Kingdom business. Help me to be a better steward over my time. In Jesus' name, I pray Amen.

But everything should be done in a fitting and orderly way.
– 1 Corinthians 14:40

Have you commanded the morning since your days began, and caused the dawn to know its place – Job 38:12

The thief comes only to steal and kill and destroy; I have come that they may have life, and have it to the full. – John 10:10

Whoever can be trusted with very little can also be trusted with much, and whoever is dishonest with very little will also be dishonest with much. – Luke16:10

So then, each of us will give an account of ourselves to God. – Romans 14:12

For we are each responsible for our own conduct. – Galatians 6:5

16
A prayer for a mentor

IT HAS BECOME COMMON FOR A LOT OF PEOPLE TO SEEK OUT a positive role model or mentor. In fact, I feel like there was a memo to the masses that read, "in order to win in life, you will need to have a mentor." If you are a professional, then I'm sure you can relate to that. You know that there's truth in that statement. Good role models and mentors are a major factor in whether or not you will succeed in life. Let's face it, no matter how good you are or how smart you are, you don't know everything. Therefore you can't teach yourself everything. Role models are people whom you admire from afar. However, a mentor is the individual who is up close and personal. They are always in your face and in your life. A mentor will take an active role in your progress and growth. A mentor will even share their own personal stories, struggles and successes.

It is most certainly good to have wise counsel and accountability in your life, however not everyone is qualified to speak in to your life. Not everyone is qualified to have a front row seat in your life. Not everyone who looks the part was assigned the role as supporting character in your life's production. That is why you must first pray. You have to pray that God connects you to the right person. Ask God to hold you back from that hungry spirit which will tempt you to chase after every person with a title, position, or money.

Let me just caution you right now from making the mistake that so many people fall into. Avoid asking someone who you don't know to speak into your life about things they may not be qualified to speak on. Avoid looking needy and hungry, reaching out for a mentor like homeless people beg for food. Instead, you should pray first and then be open to whenever God will connect you to someone who you will build a genuine relationship with. The best mentorships will come out of an organic unfolding.

I come to you Adonai my Lord
(Malachi 1:6)

Dear God, I come to you right now to thank you for being my God. I thank you God for all that you do, but specifically, I thank you for who you are. I thank you God, for your Word says that you left us a teacher who is the Holy Spirit. Now God, I lay my desires at your feet because your Word says to ask anything and I shall receive it. Lord God would you send the right people into my life right now? Lord, my heart desires a mentor who is a man or woman of God; who knows you intimately; who is a person of integrity and a person of high standards Lord, I desire to be better and I want to do better. I accept that there are those who went before me whom you have assigned to me. I welcome the one who is a smart, wise, discerning, educated, kind, giving, a good person with a sound mind. I'm open to stretching because I know it increases my capacity. Now God, help me not to be hungry or appear needy for my hope is in you for everything. Your Word says you supply all my needs. Thank God in advance for it is already done.

The way of a fool is right in his own eyes, but a wise man listens to advice. – Proverbs 12:15

Where there is no guidance, a people falls, but in an abundance of counselors there is safety. – Proverbs 11:14

Listen to advice and accept instruction, that you may gain wisdom in the future. Many are the plans in the mind of a man, but it is the purpose of the Lord that will stand. – Proverbs 19:20-21

Without counsel plans fail, but with many advisers they succeed. – Proverbs 15:22

Do not be deceived: "Bad company ruins good morals." – 1 Corinthians 15:33

17

A prayer when your health is compromised and your energy depleted

"Give all your worries and cares to God,
for he cares about you."
- 1 Peter 5:7

I HAVE HAD DAYS WHERE I WAS SO DRAINED, I COULD LITERALLY feel my blood sugar drop... or so I thought. I mean, I wasn't sleepy as much as I was exhausted, depleted and drained. As I get older, I am more in tune with my body and the vibrational signs of health and wellness versus being on the verge of a shut down if I don't get somewhere and sit down. Part of this realization came when I discovered I had anemia. I learned, at that point, how to monitor my iron levels. In fact, I learned along with low blood came low energy, lack of motivation and even low levels of depression (says my girlfriend who is NOT a medical professional but a journalist ... *GO FIGURE.*)

So the story goes that, while in the thick of life with a lot of excitement going on (as it relates to my work), I became hyper sensitive to the fact that my body wasn't showing up at 100 percent. You know how your brain has these big lofty goals to do a million things in one day but your body responds, "uhhh not today." Well that's exactly what I'm talking about. Your mind is willing but your spirit is weak and your strength is flat. One day, it got so bad, I remember saying to God on my way to Best Buy, "God help me." I had been sluggishly walking around all day and dragging my feet. I could feel that things were not working internally. So I sat in the parking lot, and I cried out right there. Then, all of sudden, I began to declare these words as if there was an award for the best performance on speaking the Word into the atmosphere. I went from a super-loud "God please" outburst to a "resist the enemy and he will flee..." declaration. Can you relate to this? Are you feeling some kind of way in your spirit about your health? Are you having a difficult time functioning at 100%? Are you running on empty? Are you concerned about your health or annoyed that you don't have enough gas to get your body moving at 100 mph? O.K., then you get it... you, too, are tired and exhausted, with little or no motivation. Maybe that's not your issue but maybe you have lost all concentration. Perhaps you're scattered in thought, unable to focus and unable to move forward. While it doesn't matter the circumstances surrounding the feeling, it does matter that you acknowledge what's happening. This is something a lot of women struggle with as we mature in age. There is a feeling in your body outside of your control affecting your ability to function at your highest level of capacity.

So let me drop this in your spirit, Greatness. You don't have to feel this way and you don't have to go about your day like a zombie. You *can* fix this. In fact, you need to address your health and wellbeing. I've had many clients struggle with accomplishing goals. Nine times of out ten, they connect their challenge to a consistent lack in energy and motivation. But you can gain an immediate shift in energy by acknowledging that you're feeling some kind of way. Then, hand it over to God. Next, you must get to the source of your not feeling 100 percent. In a lot of cases, it could be that you are just doing too much. You may have unrealistic expectations, or it could be that you are wasting time trying to do the unimaginable. But there are some instances where there's a health issue at play. When I finally went to the Doctor about my health issue, she basically said, "It's a wonder you are even able to stay awake during the day at all." My hemoglobin indicated a serious iron deficiency that was the cause of me feeling drained. One time, I was so tired, I just wanted to lay out in the street until Jesus came back. Instead, I opened up my mouth and began to look to the hills. That's what you have to do. Open up your mouth. Surrender your issue to God. Trust that He will come to your rescue as you pray. Then, you must speak and declare wellness in every area of your body, mind, soul and spirit.

I come to you Jehovah-Rapha my healer
(Exodus 15:26)

Father, in the name of Jesus, I come to you today confessing that Jesus the Christ is Lord. It is in you that I have my living, my breathing and my being. Lord, I cry out to you in this moment with all faith in You, God my healer. You are the restorer of my strength. God, I recognize my dreams, desires, goals and intentions are lofty OR [my day-to-day work load and responsibilities are many] yet I don't have enough energy to get through. So, now God I come to you, the one who made me and knit me together in my mother's womb (Psalm 139:13.) I come to you, the one who has a good plan and purpose for my life (Jeremiah 29:11.) I come to you, the one who took up our sicknesses and removed our diseases (Matthew 8:17.) God, please take whatever health issue may be luring. I believe you to block it oh God now that I come asking. I declare and decree by faith that I am covered and protected from any health threat to my livelihood. I ask you to show me the light. Let there be light in my exhausted state that I may know what you need me to know, do what you need me to do, resolve and address whatever is not according to your will. If my eating or sleeping is out of order, please Lord enable me to do these things decently and in order. If my priorities, goals and intentions are not aligned with your will, fix it, Lord. Let my priorities, goals and intentions be yours. If my roles and responsibilities are energy drainers, show me how to be responsible and fix it now Jesus. I trust you for perfect resolution. I feel you moving on my behalf. I hand it over to you. Now, I wait in great anticipation for clear instruction and a renewed spirit, a fresh wind, and a recharge. In Jesus' name, Amen.

Jesus turned, and seeing her he said, "Take heart, daughter; your faith has made you well." And instantly the woman was made well. – Matthew 9:22

And he said to him, "Rise and go your way; your faith has made you well." – Luke 17:19

And Jesus said "Everything is possible for one who believes."– Mark 9:23

Who forgives all your iniquity, who heals all your diseases? – Psalm 103:3

And he said to her, "Daughter, your faith has made you well; go in peace." While he was still speaking, someone from the ruler's house came and said, "Your daughter is dead; do not trouble the Teacher any more." But Jesus on hearing this answered him, "Do not fear; only believe, and she will be well." – Luke 8:48-50

18
A prayer when you are struggling with jealously

"For where jealousy and selfish ambition exist, there will be disorder and every vile practice."
– James 3:14-16

I DON'T THINK THERE'S A WOMAN ALIVE WHO HAS NOT HAD the issue of jealousy show up at some point in her life. We all start out from an early age looking at what the other kids have in school with a side-eye and a spirit that says, "I want thaaaaaat." It really is just a natural part of human nature to see something you like or love or to see something that just calls your name and you want it for yourself. That was my story growing up, but thank God, with personal development work and prayer, I got over it. Now I can't say that I never find myself wanting something that belongs to someone else (don't judge me), but I can say that God has helped me through it.

If you were to tell the truth about the spirit of jealously, I'm sure there's been a time when you looked at someone with envy who seemed to have no struggle and no worry about their bills, rent/mortgage, love life, children, job, work or anything. I'm sure you can remember a time when you witnessed someone having a big win in their life and you pretended to be happy when deep down you were thinking "why not me." It's O.K. It happens. It's part of our makeup until we "unlearn" the natural urge to want what others have. It is a command of God: do not covet your neighbors' things (Exodus 20:17.)

Well, let me drop this in your spirit. You are not alone. I've been there and truth be told, no matter how much stuff you have in life, you'll never get over wanting more. But the catch is that, often times, more so it happens to belong to someone else! Now let's bring balance to this conversation. There's nothing wrong with admiring what another person has. The problem is, when the emotional charge hits your spirit, and that admiration turns into jealously. You must be careful. Your outer disposition might fool some people, but Luke 16:15 says, "God knows your heart." So you cannot hide your thoughts from Him. You can pretend to be happy and supportive all you want, but God sees all things. You would never want God to see how ungrateful you are and how your lack of faith is indicative of your jealously of others. Even if you are not where you want to be in life, give thanks in all things (1 Thessalonians 5:18) and be content in all circumstances (Philippians 4:11.) Contentment and gratitude may bring the release you need for God to send the overflow in your life.

In order for you to position yourself to receive the blessing of God, you must be grateful for what you already have. In your gratitude, you will become a better steward over what God as already given you. If God can trust you with a little, the Word says He will entrust you with more. Learn how to move to a place of gratitude for others. But make sure that jealously doesn't slip in. Once you have prayed and asked God to release the spirit of jealously from you, you will need to actively work on it. Whenever you find yourself watching another in envy, thank God for that individual. God may have brought them into your life to stretch your imagination and to give you a vision of what's possible for you. Instead of being hateful of that person, be thankful. Thank God for blessing that person so they can be a blessing to you.

I come to you God my Keeper
(Psalm 121:5)

Father God in the name of Jesus, I come to you right now to confess. I am overwhelmed with feelings of jealously. Your Word says "do not covet anything that belongs to someone else" (Exodus 20:17) and I want to be obedient to that.

I can't help myself, but I know Your Word says, "If I ask anything, it will be done." I ask right now for a release from the spirit of jealously. Lord, take away my wandering eyes, thoughts and obsessions. Transform my mind according to your Word in Romans 12:2, so I can think like you think and speak forth the abundant life you have for me (John 10:10.) Move me out of jealousy and envy. Give me the spirit of love and appreciation for others. Would you please release the strong emotion of negativity and hate in me? Increase my positivity quotient. Help me to delight in you always. Help me Lord to be genuinely happy for others and to become a woman so confident that nothing will disrupt my spirit. Hold my tongue, Lord, at the mere gesture to spread gossip or tear down another woman.

I now step into a new season of growing into the woman you have called me to be. I declare a release of everything you are holding up for me upon my release of everything that is distracting me. God, thank you for enabling me to keep my eyes on you. I will not turn to the left or to the right. Thank you for being my Jehovah Jireh, the Lord who provides in good measure, pressed down, shaken together, running over, and placed in my lap, Hallelujah (Luke 6:38.) Amen.

Take delight in the LORD, and he will give you the desires of your heart. – Psalm 37:4

Do not conform to the pattern of this world, but be transformed by the renewing of your mind. Then you will be able to test and approve what God's will is--his good, pleasing and perfect will. – Romans 12:2

But if you have bitter jealousy and selfish ambition in your hearts, do not boast and be false to the truth. This is not the wisdom that comes down from above, but is earthly, unspiritual, and demonic. For where jealousy and selfish ambition exist, there will be disorder and every vile practice. – James 3:14-16

A tranquil heart gives life to the flesh, but envy makes the bones rot. – Proverbs 14:30

Do nothing from rivalry or conceit, but in humility count others more significant than yourselves. – Philippians 2:3

19

A prayer for job change/transition

> "*The LORD will open the heavens, the storehouse of his bounty, to send rain on your land in season and to bless all the work of your hands. You will lend to many nations but will borrow from none.*"
> **– Deuteronomy 28:12**

O H GOD. MY NIECE SENT ME A TEXT EARLY IN THE MORNING while I was out doing my 4 miles and immediately I clinch up. Nobody calls me this early. This is my sacred morning time so whenever there's a call, I know something's up. She says "can you talk ....I'm about to leave my job ASAP." Of course I call her right away and we have a discussion about a major decision she's about to make. She got an offer for an amazing job. Turns out this is exactly what she wants to do! She's currently working at a job that most would think is the "everything" in New York City in the thick of things for a major brand that comes with a certain kind of prestige, celebrity access, and music entertainment (all things most young people salivate over.) However an opportunity is presented to her and she's ready to move on it. Her resignation letter is prepared, signed, and sealed but not yet delivered.

She walks me through background information about the new opportunity and her current situation. At the end of our chat, I said, "I am happy for you and so proud of you because you make good decisions." That was the truth after hearing her thought process. Three things in particular stood out. She mentioned that she had prayed to God and asked for clarity. Then she said of the two opportunities, this offer was the one that she would do for free. Lastly she made the distinction between the two opportunities and which one fit her ideal lifestyle. That was a wow moment for me.

Here is a young woman who gets it. She's young and she's smart. She prays, thinks things through, is in tune with her heart and she knows what she desires in life. Most of all, she's willing to go after her dreams in spite of resistance. This is the substance of what most parents would want for their children. What an awesome testament to her mother and father. This kind of substance and greatness only comes from God. So, woman of God, let me drop this in your spirit. If you are in a place having to make a decision about your job, let me encourage you to do what the young 25-year-old did. Whenever you are transitioning, and whenever there is an opportunity before you, never make a hasty decision. Sleep on it. Take a day or two to really get clarity and direction. When you move too swiftly, you don't get to think things through. When you don't think things through, you don't make the best decisions. When you step away from the excitement of what's before you, you are able to present the opportunity to God and seek Him for clarity, guidance and direction. The Word of the Lord says, "Seek first the kingdom of God" and this is what it looks like to seek God. Seeking God in this instance means that you realize how badly you want something, but you're willing to step away from it in order to present it to God first. Then you contemplate the opportunity based on what you want in life. It is perfectly fine, fair and reasonable for you to make a decision about a job opportunity based on your heart, passion and purpose. Lastly, you have every right to want what you want and to have what you want. In other words, if your rigid corporate conservative 9 to 5 job does not align with who you are and who God created you to be, then find the environment that supports you, fuels you, and adds to your life. You have permission to make decisions based on how you want to live. The problem with so many people struggling with their jobs is they find themselves working somewhere that doesn't align with their ideal life blueprint. Now there will be naysayers who will say you can't have a job doing what you love, but that's nonsense. It makes no sense for you to be a child of the Most High God and not be able to have what you desire. Stop playing by the world's rules and trust God for everything. His Word says, "I came to give you life that you may have it to the full." (John 10:10.)

I come to you El-Olam
Everlasting God
(Psalm 90_1-3)

Father God in the name of Jesus, I come before you right now to say thank you. Thank you God for your favor upon my life. I realize that so many people are unemployed or underemployed. Many people are working at jobs that give them no options. But you have given me options and opportunities, favor, promotions and increase. Thank you, Lord. I don't want to move without you, so, please, take my hand. Guide me in the direction that you would have me to go. I recognize that there is an awesome opportunity before me, and now I have come to a crossroads. I am ready to move on this amazing opportunity, but I choose to seek you first. Grant me the discernment and wisdom to make the right decision. I pray for my current employer and everyone whom you have assigned me to ...those who support my rise and shine, and those who don't. Make it plain. Protect, guard and keep me in the palm of your hands. Hold me to your standard and keep me humble. Give me the skill, talent and ability to outperform. And when it is all said and done, even now, I will forever give your name the praise, the honor, and the glory in Jesus' name...Amen.

..teaching them to observe all that I commanded you; and lo, I am with you always, even to the end of the age. – Matthew 28:20

Take delight in the LORD, and he will give you the desires of your heart. – Psalm 37:4

Now faith is confidence in what we hope for and assurance about what we do not see. – Hebrews 11:1

Be strong and courageous. Do not fear or be in dread of them, for it is the Lord your God who goes with you. He will not leave you or forsake you." – Deuteronomy 31:6

For God gave us a spirit not of fear but of power and love and self-control. – 2 Timothy 1:7

Have I not commanded you? Be strong and courageous. Do not be frightened, and do not be dismayed, for the Lord your God is with you wherever you go." – Joshua 1:9

20

A prayer when you are struggling with procrastination

"Whatever you do, work heartily,
as for the Lord and not for men... "
– Colossians 3:23

I PROMISE YOU, ALTHOUGH THIS TOPIC MAY NOT BE ON TOP OF your prayer list, it needs to be if you struggle with procrastination like me. I mean, this thing right here required a divine move of God himself to show up and fix me.

My dirty little secret that I struggled with for so long was the issue of putting off, stalling, deferring, and postponing stuff; from big to small, meaningless to significant. My dirty little secret was hidden behind closed doors for many years. In that closet were bags filled with procrastination. For many years, I rarely went to the mailbox. It wasn't a regular routine for me. I had no system or structure. The only consistent thing I did was choose to consistently put off walking to the mailbox to avoid dealing with what was inside. I was such a procrastinator that I had several rounds of checks written out to me via snail mail yet they had expired long before I got them to the Bank. They were caught up first in the mailbox. Then they sat on the kitchen table. Then they migrated over to a bag and then a closet, and eventually, I tackled it on those rare occasions that I got a burst of energy or the motivation to be responsible. The expired checks had to be the breaking point, however, and one of the biggest lessons on my journey.

In this teachable moment, the most profound lesson was this: God was trying to bless me but I was standing in my own way. This was a big AHA moment. It fueled me to do better and then help other women do the same. Out of my own messiness I gave birth to a program called "Girlfriends Pray Life Camp." The mission is to provide abundant living resources for women. One of the signature programs "James Girls" teaches women how to get out of your own way and position yourself for abundance. In other words, "James Girls" would have been the resource I needed for "how to" stop being reckless, how to better and how to position myself for all that God has for me (like those checks that were coming in the mail.)

If you resonate with my story, it's probably because you too put off things or you're challenged with consistency. It may be that you put off opening your mail, balancing your check book, paying bills or dealing with your personal business matters. It could be that you have stalled from pursuing a hobby, getting a license/degree, or writing a book. Maybe you have a project that you started but you can't seem to finish. Whatever it is, procrastination is real. In some instances, it may not come with an obvious cost but in a lot of instances your delay may come with a hefty price tag. It can cost you money, time, opportunities and even your freedom.

In order to stop procrastinating, first acknowledge it is real. It is a form of resistance, a force within us, intended to keep us small. Next, make a list of what procrastination is costing you so you can feel the feeling and allow that emotion to motivate you to action. One time, I attempted to address my issue with procrastination by calling procrastinators anonymous. After speaking to them, I was relieved to discover that other people were dealing with the issue. I tried it a few times, but my inconsistency got in the way. And it wasn't until I had a real comprehensive solution that included practical work and prayer that I began to see a change in my life. You have to understand procrastination, be aware of its costs and then, you need a word from the Lord. Once I got a word from the Lord on this matter, freedom was a non-negotiable. That word from the Lord was simple: do all things decently and in order. That was God's way of saying, "Dee, you can't operate in anything other than excellence because that's who you are...excellent." Once you know it's a command of God that we move responsibly through life in all we do, that's when you will find your breakthrough and your release.

Let me drop this in your spirit. Nothing is too hard for God. God is for you, but the enemy will try to use delays and distractions to throw you off task and to keep you from Kingdom business. The busier you are, the more you will have to do. But be careful of the bright and shiny objects that exist in the world (like Facebook, Twitter, and Instagram) because if you're not careful, these simple distractions will help to facilitate your fall into the enemy's trap. If you want to resolve anything in your life, you have to go to the Word of God. See what the Lord has to say about the matter. Procrastination is a tool of the enemy. Its underlying purpose is a scheme that intends to strip away your responsibility for your life. The enemy's hope is that it will keep you from pursuing the call and purpose on your life. Stephen Pressfield once said, "Procrastination is a form of resistance and resistance is an internal force to keep you small." Don't allow procrastination to keep you small. You are better than how you are living right now. God has a plan and a purpose for your life. Don't allow procrastination to cancel out the opportunity that is before you. Take a stand and declare that you are responsible. Decree that you will do all things on time. Then, create a plan. Learn to manage your life like you run a business. Use systems and deadlines to move out of neutral. Finally, tell someone about your goals and deadlines so they can hold you accountable. If you do this, you will most certainly step into the next best version of who God has created you to be. You can do this!

I come to you Alpha and Omega
(Revelation 22:13)

Father, in the name of Jesus, I come to you right now confessing that I have not been responsible with my time. Lord God, I confess that I have not been effective in managing my life and taking ownership of my responsibilities. Lord, whether there is an internal block or I've just been lazy or unwilling to do my work, I confess right now and ask you for forgiveness. For every delay in or lack of responsibility, not showing up on time, not handling my personal matters, not paying my bills, dealing with mail, outstanding debts, organizing my life, I turn to You. For every delay I've created by not stepping up to who you have created me to be, like not working on my growth and development, not going deeper in my spiritual walk, not furthering my education or fully stepping into my purpose and gifting, I turn to you. God, for every delay in being an ambassador for you in good deeds, projects and initiatives like volunteering my time to those in need, I turn to you. God for every delay in reconciling open and unresolved issues of my past, I turn to you. God for every delay in being a good steward over my body like getting to preventative care appointments on time or resolving health concerns in a timely manner, I turn to you. Help me Lord to do everything as unto you. (Colossians 3:23.) Help me to show up decently and in order in all that I do (1 Corinthians 14:40.) I declare and decree idleness has no place in my life. I will, from this point forward, be obedient to your Word according to James 1:22 which says, "Be a doer of the word and not a hearer alone, or I am only deceiving myself." So every word spoken into my spirit through this prayer,

I declare: I am now a doer of your Word. I shall move in action knowing that if and when I fall, Lord, you will be there to get me back on track. In Jesus' name, I ask you Lord and consider it done...Amen.

Whatever you do, work heartily, as for the Lord and not for men,
– Colossians 3:23

But be doers of the word, and not hearers only, deceiving yourselves. – James 1:22

For we hear that some among you walk in idleness, not busy at
work, but busybodies. Now such persons we command and encourage in the Lord Jesus Christ to do their work quietly and to earn
their own living. – 2 Thessalonians 3:11-12

That the man of God may be competent, equipped for every good
work. – 2 Timothy 3:17

Love not sleep, lest you come to poverty; open your eyes, and you
will have plenty of bread. – Proverbs 20:13

How long will you lie there, O sluggard? When will you arise from
your sleep? – Proverbs 6:9

21

A prayer when you're dealing with negative people

> "Do not be misled:
> 'Bad company corrupts good character.'"
> – **1 Corinthians 15:33**

"IT WAS LITERALLY ONE OF THE MOST DISAPPOINTING conversations I've ever had with my mother..."

Have you ever had some really exciting news or something really amazing happen to you? Have you ever received an opportunity of a life-time and it was exactly what you wanted? If so, imagine yourself back there in that moment. What would you do if the first person you called to share the news with, was the very person who squashed your dreams? In one talk, they killed your dreams like a trained assassin. It could be your husband, your partner, your sister, your girlfriend, your mother, your father, or your child. The person you respect the most is the person whose opinion matters to you more than anything; and it is that person who is both for you and against you.

I received a message like this from a young woman and my heart just sank. I knew that it was a blow that she was not prepared to take. Although she was a mature young woman, she had yet to make sense of why the person closest to her had to find everything wrong with what she believed was 100% right for her life. She had yet to figure out how to manage a relationship with someone who was on the one hand, close to her, but on the other hand, not on the same page with her. It's sad when people who claim to love you, build a case against you. It's sad when people go out of their way to find a reason to argue against your dreams. This scenario becomes a recurring theme for so many, however part of the reason it keeps showing up in your life is because you allow it to happen. People who speak against you do it because you teach people how to treat you. No one can speak against you unless you give them center stage access to perform and a microphone to project. I have to admit, as a young woman, I can remember seeking others approval. However, as I grew older and more secure in who God created me to be, I became less concerned about other people's opinions. In other words, I became discerning and discriminate. Certainly, you can seek counsel from certifiably wise people, but even in that scenario, make sure to hold up their opinion to the standard of God's word: "whatever things are true; whatever things are noble; whatever things are righteous; whatever things are excellent; whatever things are noteworthy; whatever things are praiseworthy; whatever things are positive…think on such things."

So let me drop this in your spirit. You don't need permission from other people when God has already given you His approval. You don't need anyone else to agree with you. You don't even need anyone else to see what you see. Other people are not seeing out of the lens that God gave you. T.D. Jakes describes how you can share space with your loved ones, but still not see things the same way. He explained, "If you are a giraffe sharing space with a turtle, your perspective will be different because you are not on the same level. Even though you may share space with a turtle, a giraffe will definitely see things differently because his perspective is higher. What you see is based on your level. So stop wasting time trying to win people over to your ideas. You are going to hurt your neck bending down to talk to them (turtles.) Love them from afar but be clear with your boundaries. Stand guarded with who has permission to speak into your life. When people speak *to* you *about* you, understand that more often than not, it has nothing to do *with* you. People think, people speak and people act based on the lenses they are wearing. Don Miguel, in his book *The Four Agreements* says "don't take anything personal. It's not about you. What someone says about you says more about them than it does about you." Listen to God. Follow your heart. And walk with these words on your lips: "I trust you, God."

I come to you Everlasting Father
(Isaiah 9:6)

Father God in the name of Jesus, I come before you right now to lift up [name the negative person]. Lord I know you see all things and I ask that you come and see about this unfortunate situation. It's wearing me down to be in the same space with constant negativity. This person speaks against my dreams, doubts my desires and it is very difficult to handle. Now God, can you step into an out-of-control challenge? Work through whatever issue is in them, and then God, if it's me, move me out of my own way. I thank you for your grace, mercy and favor. I thank you for working out my flaws and making me into the woman that you have called me to be. Help me to stay positive. Help me to become more optimistic. Thank you for showing me who I don't want to be. Thank you for clarifying who I need to be and how I can be a better encourager of others. Lord, send me light in the way of good people who see the best in me and want the best for me. Send me positive, like-minded people. Help me to resolve this issue between the pessimist in my house, circle, or family. Begin the pruning process right now. Get rid of every dead thing that means me no good. Your word says, "Bad company corrupts good character." So Lord, I ask that you remove all of those who are against me. Release into my life right now a seasoned mentor\role model\coach\sponsor\covering that would genuinely build me up and support me. Then, show me how to pay it forward. In Jesus' Name. Amen

But I say to you that everyone who is angry with his brother will be liable to judgment; whoever insults his brother will be liable to the council; and whoever says, 'You fool!' will be liable to the hell of fire. – Matthew 5:22

Fathers, do not provoke your children to anger, but bring them up in the discipline and instruction of the Lord. – 1 John 4:8

Anyone who does not love does not know God, because God is love. – Philippians 2:1-30

So if there is any encouragement in Christ, any comfort from love, any participation in the Spirit, any affection and sympathy, complete my joy by being of the same mind, having the same love, being in full accord and of one mind. Do nothing from rivalry or conceit, but in humility count others more significant than yourselves. Let each of you look not only to his own interests, but also to the interests of others. Have this mind among yourselves, which is yours in Christ Jesus, – Philippians 2:4

Treat others the same way you want them to treat you. – Luke 6:31

22

A prayer when you are struggling with sexual temptation

> "No temptation has overtaken you that is not common to man. God is faithful, and he will not let you be tempted beyond your ability, but with the temptation he will also provide the way of escape, that you may be able to endure it."
> – *1 Corinthians 10:13*

I DON'T KNOW ABOUT YOU, BUT IF I CAN BE BRUTALLY HONEST, I love the love of a man. I love the presence of a man, the connection with a man, the covering and the yummy intimate relationships that one can only have with a man. Certainly, I believe that the highest level of a love relationship, is the union of marriage. God is absolutely *for* marriage, and so am I. However, the challenge is great if you are a single woman. How do you manage the desire for relationship with the temptation to wander down the dating path when there is no commitment? This is one of the most difficult challenges I believe for a single woman, but I know from personal experience that God is the only way that you can manage through this kind of temptation.

I'll never forget when one of my girlfriends, during the height of a purpose-filled season, had an accidental slip with a man. She was walking through every door that God had opened for her, and then, out of nowhere (or so it seemed), there came a knock at the door. It was her ex! He came in, and the next thing she knew, they were having hot, heated, and heavily passionate sex (actually I don't know the details, but you can imagine what happens when men and women get together)! Well, the next day, she was absolutely broken up about it. She knew that she had disappointed God, and that was the source of her heartbreak. She wasn't worried about what other people would think or say. She wasn't even concerned about the ex and whether or not there would be a relationship. Here was a woman who had been clearly walking with the Lord; so much so, that she felt convicted in her spirit. So, I got on the phone right away to release her from the grips of the enemy. Even though she knew she was out of order in the eyes of God, I wanted her to know that she was not out of the kingdom. God doesn't throw us away for our mistakes. God doesn't disown us for committing a sin. If we confess our sins, he is faithful and just to forgive us of our sins and purify us from all unrighteousness (1 John 1:9.) Now the enemy was working to win her because she was a threat. She was doing the work of the Lord, and of course, he didn't like that.

In situations like this, can I just pause and say: it's helpful to have good quality sister friends who you can trust to pray with you during times like these. You need people who will not gossip about you, but sisters who will speak life into your spirit and allow themselves to be used to pull you out of the grips of the enemy. God uses people. For that reason, positive like-minded women ought to stay together. There is so much that we share in common, especially as it pertains to our temptations and thorns.

Now the reason I could speak to her situation was not just because I work with women and minister to women, it's because

I've been there. I've had personal slip-ups and I've even fallen into things I shouldn't have. Yes, I have made many mistakes myself, but over time, as I matured in Christ, I learned the lesson and never had to take that class again. I knew I had learned the lesson of not allowing my own desires to be with Mr. Tall, Dark and Handsome when I truly surrendered a potential relationship to the Lord. After a short window of time, the relationship plummeted from hot to cold. I knew then that God had shown up to save me from myself. This situation carried such a strong vibrational frequency and the connection was undeniable! But what I love the most is that God matured me to such an extent that I could discern when the vibrational frequency was too high for me to handle on my own. Some women, or shall I say some younger versions of myself, might have believed that the Spirit of God was telling me to pursue this relationship because I had a strong vibrational frequency with him. But no, it wasn't that. It was just that there was an assignment on my life. And with every assignment, there is a level of sacrifice required in order to operate at 100%. Sometimes, you've got to be willing to let go of what looks good in order to pursue God. It's a powerful lesson I learned from Toure Roberts, author of the book *Purpose Awakening*, when he speaks of his relationship. He said "Be willing to surrender the thing you love if it's not God's Will."

I decided that I am so serious about my walk with the Lord, that nothing is worth interrupting the frequency between me and my God. He is so good to me! He is so good to us! Nothing is worth me risking this yummy relationship that I have with God, so I will try my best to get this thing right. *Now let's keep it real.* It has taken me just about a lifetime to get where I am today, and I am still working at this walk. But, that encounter with Mr. Tall, Black and Handsome that would've been clearly outside of the will of God, really converted me. I'm a witness that God will show up and provide a way of escape when you go to Him with a sincere heart and when you ask Him for help.

So let me drop this in your spirit, woman of God. Whenever you find yourself in a compromising situation that may conflict with who you are, you don't have to be strong. Dad will step in and *be* your strength. It is written, "My grace is sufficient for you; my power is made perfect in weakness" (2 Corinthians 12:9.) Let God be God in that moment. Surrender your weakness to God and expect Him to show up and rescue you. God knows your weakness. God knows your struggle. He knows when Mr. tall, dark and handsome is only going to lead you into something that will be a temporary moment of instant gratification. Tell the truth and you will shame the devil. Let's try it right here. I know I shouldn't be with Mr. tall, dark and handsome, but I honestly might have let him "have it" if it was not for God and the God in me. I knew if I was going to stand my ground, it would have to be by God's divine move.

So ask God to move in you right now. Ask God to move in your *"complicated non-relationship."* Ask God to release you from the fatal attraction if it's not His will for you to be in a committed marital relationship with Mr. tall, dark and handsome. You are not the first woman who has gone through this. Whether you slept with Mr. tall dark and handsome in a moment of heated passion, or somehow, by divine intervention, God stepped in and turn hot to cold. Either way, the Bible is true: "No temptation has overtaken you that is not common to man..." (1 Corinthians 10:13.) You can do it, woman of God. You can keep your panties on in the name of Jesus. Don't allow a moment of passion to cancel the call on your life.

I come to you my Deliverer
(Romans 11:26)

Father, in the name of Jesus, I come before you right now, God, asking for a way of escape. Lord, I'm struggling with temptation but I believe you now for self-control. I know that you would not command me to do anything that you haven't already enabled me to do. Because the fruit of the Spirit is evidenced by self-control, I ask you right now to make Your Word a reality in my heart. Teach me self-control so that my fleshly desires will not cause me to sin against you. Father, your eyes saw my unformed body when I was made in a secret place. Therefore, you know how you knit me together in my mother's womb. I am a woman; emotionally guided, but often sexually stimulated when I am in the presence of a man. I don't want to lose you in a moment of heat. I don't want to be inappropriate. I declare and decree that you are my standard, oh God. I believe and live by Your Word in Philippians 4:9, which instructs me to follow you. I thank you for making me a quality woman of integrity walking out 1 Corinthians 14:40 which says "do all things decently and in order." Enable me to resist. I want what you want for me and if he is not it, move [insert name] out of the picture. Give me discernment, clarity and solid, unshakable faith. In Jesus' name, Amen.

No temptation has overtaken you that is not common to man. God is faithful, and he will not let you be tempted beyond your ability, but with the temptation he will also provide the way of escape, that you may be able to endure it. – 1 Corinthians 10:13

But I say, walk by the Spirit, and you will not gratify the desires of the flesh. Galatians 5:16

Flee from sexual immorality. Every other sin a person commits is outside the body, but the sexually immoral person sins against his own body. Or do you not know that your body is a temple of the Holy Spirit within you, whom you have from God? You are not your own, for you were bought with a price. So glorify God in your body. – 1 Corinthians 6:18-20

For because he himself has suffered when tempted, he is able to help those who are being tempted. – Hebrews 2:18

So whoever knows the right thing to do and fails to do it, for him it is sin. – James 4:17

23

A prayer for family reconciliation

I T IS A SMART THING TO DO AND A BIBLICAL MANDATE FROM God: to reconcile estranged relationships with family members. It doesn't matter who did what. It doesn't matter if you were offended or if you did the offending. The right thing to do in the eyes of God, is to reconcile immediately. God takes it very seriously how we treat others. If it weren't true, then it wouldn't be the second commandment. The Bible makes an excellent case for why it is so important to have healthy relationships with other people. The Lord challenges us in so many ways on this particular issue. The consistent theme as believers is to love God, trust God, and respect God enough to love those whom we can see every day. In fact, our love for God is proven in our ability to love our neighbor. It's impossible to say you love Him if you harbor anger, hatred and unforgiveness in your heart towards another. His Word clearly states, "How can you love me who you haven't seen yet hate your brother who you see." (1 John 4:20)

The one thing that I see among many families (that is completely mind blowing, if you ask me) is the level of disrespect or disregard among family members. For instance, have you ever had an argument with a family member who fights with words like "F *** you, Mother F, B****" Have you ever witnessed families whose common language and weapons of war are words of death and destruction? They say things like, "go to hell, I hope you die, kiss my ..." Or, maybe you have been in a situation with someone in your family who fights dirty. Maybe it's typical of your family to say hurtful things without using expletives. Is it possible that your family is one who engages in talking behind your back, stirring up the pot, opening a can of worms with no regard to how hurtful it can be? Bottom line is this: all of that is wrong on so many levels. But the thing that gets me most is the fact that we say things to our family members, the people we love, that we would never say to our employers, neighbors or strangers we meet on the street! It is not just words, but our behaviors and actions that make us guilty as well. We will walk in a room without saying hello. We will not answer a question when asked, or we will give someone the cold shoulder and ignore them while they are speaking.

This may not speak to everyone reading, but I know it is speaking to someone. If there is a tug in your heart right now because of some dissension in your family, I want to encourage you. You are in the right place to take on the posture of prayer. You are in the right place to just humble yourself and acknowledge that your heart is hurting for whatever is happening in your family. Whether your sister, brother, mother, or father abandoned you, disowned you, disrespected you or disregarded you, there is still a call to acknowledge what happened and to take it to the throne. The pain we feel when our family does something dishonorable,

132

is one hundred times greater than a stranger on the street. We expect more from the people we love (and we should.) However, the greater accountability lies on you, my sister in Christ. Why? Because God expects more from you.

So let me drop this in your spirit. Resolve whatever issue you have with your family. Whoever is responsible for the offense should have no bearing on you being a woman of God. Once you know better, you have to do better. The Lord does not take kind to believers who claim to be Christian, but somehow behave contrary to God's Word. Leviticus 19 says "do not nurse hatred in your heart for any of your relatives. Confront people directly so you will not be held guilty for their sin." It may be easier to forgive in your heart and more difficult to confront your relative, however trust that God will be with you. Know that you have the Word of God on your side. "If your brother or sister sins against you, rebuke them and if they repent, forgive them" (Luke 17:3.) God forgave you, so you are to forgive those who have offended you. You don't want to be a hypocrite. God will honor your heart if you sincerely go to the throne of grace on their behalf. God loves you in spite of the pain you might be dealing with right now. Know that you can get through this. God is the friend that sticks closer than a brother (Proverbs 18:24.) Whatever you do, reconcile the issues that you have between your family members. Turn to the Word of God in everything that you do. Now that you are seeking God and his will for your life, be kind, tenderhearted and forgiving as God in Heaven forgave you (Ephesians 4:32.)

I come to you Jehovah-Gmoloah God of Recompense
(Jeremiah 51:6)

Father, in the name of Jesus, I come before you right now because I need you. I'm heavy in my heart, and at times, I am even overwhelmed with sorrow about my family. Lord, I don't know where I went wrong. I don't know why this is so difficult. I don't know how to move forward, but I do have enough sense to turn to you. I don't want to be a hypocrite. I want to be the woman that you have called me to be. I want to show up decently and in order according to Your Word in 1 Corinthians 14:40. I believe with your power that I can be the best ambassador for you and my family. Use me, God, to be an example. I want to represent you in the best way possible. Help me to forgive as Christ forgave me. Would you please soften my heart according to Your Word in Ephesians 4:32? Help me to be kind and tenderhearted. Help me to be patient. Release me from the spirit of envy, rage, and arrogance. Allow my love to overrule my need to be right. Allow your love in me to override my stubbornness and unforgiving spirit. Thank you, Lord, for Your Word in Matthew 18 that encourages me to go and speak to [name it]. I believe you to enable me to give a soft answer in order to diffuse any anger that may be present.

Lord, I'm believing you for reconciliation. I know that nothing is too hard for you. Now God, I declare and decree a divine shift in every relationship that is strained. Let your will be done in my life. Bless each and every one of my family members, my friends, my enemies, the naysayers and the haters. Bless them, God. Turn my heart towards them that you might get the glory. In Jesus' name, Amen.

Children, obey your parents in the Lord, for this is right. "Honor your father and mother" (this is the first commandment with a promise), "that it may go well with you and that you may live long in the land." Fathers, do not provoke your children to anger, but bring them up in the discipline and instruction of the Lord. – Ephesians 6:1-4

You shall not hate your brother in your heart, but you shall reason frankly with your neighbor, lest you incur sin because of him. You shall not take vengeance or bear a grudge against the sons of your own people, but you shall love your neighbor as yourself: I am the Lord. – Leviticus 19:17-18

Be kind to one another, tenderhearted, forgiving one another, as God in Christ forgave you. Ephesians 4:32

If your brother sins against you, go and tell him his fault, between you and him alone. If he listens to you, you have gained your brother. But if he does not listen, take one or two others along with you, that every charge may be established by the evidence of two or three witnesses. If he refuses to listen to them, tell it to the church. And if he refuses to listen even to the church, let him be to you as a Gentile and a tax collector. – Matthew 18:15-17

Whoever claims to love God yet hates a brother or sister is a liar. For whoever does not love their brother and sister, whom they have seen, cannot love God, whom they have not seen – 1 John 4:20 NIV

24

A prayer when you want God to fix your life

> *"You were taught, with regard to your former way of life, to put off your old self, which is being corrupted by its deceitful desires;"*
> *— Ephesians 4:22*

I F YOU'RE PRAYING FOR GOD TO FIX YOUR LIFE AND WAITING for it to just magically happen, I've got news for you. *This is a public service announcement.* You cannot just sit back and wait for everything to be done *for* you. Now you may already know this, however the truth of the matter is that many people know a lot of things but they don't always walk *in* that knowledge. In other words, you may know that you can't just delegate God to do things for you without any effort or action on your part, but very often, we go to God in prayer, drop off our petitions like dirty clothes in a Laundromat, and then do absolutely nothing to line up our actions with what we believe.

The good news is, if you are looking to God for everything, then you are off to a great start! You are absolutely 100% allowed and invited to do so. The Word of the Lord says, "You have not because you ask not." The Lord says that we can ask anything according to his will and it will be done. God tells us to ask and he wants us to be totally dependent upon Him. However, this also means that we are not to look outside of ourselves for others to do for us what God wants to do. "Others" includes our employer, our parents, our husbands and friends. Rather, we are to trust God for everything. Very often, where we go wrong is in two main areas. First, we must trust God for everything, and that includes honoring His Word about all things. In other words, be careful not to ask God to fix things in your life, but when it comes to God's commands, you neglect that which God has called you to fix. For instance, have you ever asked God to fix your marriage but you're holding onto unforgiveness? Have you ever asked God to fix your job situation, but you disregard and disrespect your employer? Have you ever asked God to fix your health, but then you turn around and consume things that might be harmful to your body? My point is simple. Very often, we ask God to fix things and then we don't take Him at His Word regarding the role we are to play in order for those things to be fixed. John 14:15 says, "If you love me, you will obey what I command." (NIV.) If anyone claims to love God, then he or she will obey His teachings. But the hard truth is, when we don't obey Him, we show up as hypocritical believers. When we say we love the Lord, but we don't honor his teaching, then we deny his lordship in our lives. The Word says, "Why do you call me Lord Lord when you don't do what I say? (Luke 6:46.) God cautions us from being merely hearers of the Word, but not doers of the Word (James 1:22.)

The other area where we fall short is asking God to fix our lives and not taking any personal responsibility to act. It's a good thing to want to do better and be better. It's a good thing to turn to the Lord and ask God to fix your situation. It's a good thing to have faith and trust in the Lord to move mountains on your behalf. However, it's an unreasonable thing for you to believe that you can just sit back and do nothing while God moves on your behalf. Yes, it's true that God performs miracles. Yes, it's true that God doesn't operate like man, or in a way that He requires us to do something in order to get something. He does, however, require us to be obedient to His Word. It's not that we have to do *this* in order to gain *that*. No, that's science. That's not necessarily God. At the same time, God's Word is clear: faith without a corresponding action is dead. In other words, faith by itself does not produce results.

A prime example of this command is when I was working to clear up my credit. I had no outstanding issues, but my credit score was still low. In having a conversation with a woman knowledgeable in the area, she said that the creditors should've removed those blemishes off of my record between a certain window of time, however they didn't. So in order to fix the problem, I had to submit a letter asking them to remove it. Then, I would win. But the words she said after giving me wise, financial counsel, stuck with me. She said, "Nothing will happen unless and until you take action." In other words, my issue would not resolve itself. My issue was one that could be fixed. But it would not just fix itself. It was as fundamental as elementary school mathematics. I didn't need God to miraculously increase my credit if there was action I could take on my own behalf, within the realm of personal responsibility and capability, as a believer. In the same way, let me drop this into your spirit, my sister. The issue that is in front of you right now is resolvable. Even though it may feel like you've been struggling for a long time, this is not permanent! This is not the end of your story. However big or small your issue may be; and however deep a hole you may be in, God is able to fix your situation. But you, my friend, must move! Even though you may be going through what feels like a 40-year-long wilderness, you can overcome this. Even though it feels like the world is against you, and even though you feel like you need a right now quick-fix,

I want you to know, God is able. It is going to take work. You're going to have to do something. God made you a human being capable of working in the flow of God. So all things are possible to those who believe. Your heavenly Father wants you to call on Him. He wants you to believe Him for the impossible, not for the doable. The Word of the Lord shares insight on the spirit of laziness, which leads to poverty. While the one who works hard is the one who will become wealthy (Proverbs 10:4.) So, stop delegating your fixes to the Lord as if He is a repair shop. Know that God will do his part *when* you do your part!

I come to you God Almighty
(Genesis 17:1)

Father, in the name of Jesus, I come to say forgive me Lord for any offense in my prayers of petition. I know Lord that my primary objective in prayer is to come close to you, oh Lord. Forgive me if I have come, in the past, asking for things without a posture of gratitude. I come to you to be with you, and to thank you for life. I am seeking clarity from you as it pertains to fixing my life in the area if [name it_____]. I thank you Lord that you allow me to come to you with everything and all things when I am weary and burdened. I thank you that in Matthew 11:28, your promise to give me rest still stands. I thank you Lord that you allow me to come to you as my source and my provider for every need (Philippians 4:19.) I thank you that I don't have to depend on flesh (Psalms 118:8), because I can depend on you. Now, God, I ask for your help in stepping fully into total reliance over other areas in my life, like my job, my parents, my spouse, and other concerns that only you know about.

In my total reliance of you, please forgive me if, in my prayers, I have pressed you on all sides just to supply my needs. Forgive me, Lord for overlooking your commands. Please show me the errors of my ways, oh God, so that I might seek you for forgiveness and repent. God I accept your Word cautioning me not to simply be a hearer of Your Word, but also a doer of the Word (James 1:22.) I believe your Word, which reminds me that faith without a corresponding action is dead (James 2:14.) God, help me to take appropriate action over the areas where my responsibility is lacking. I don't want to move out of your will. I know I must take personal responsibility for my life. I declare that I am a new creature. Take complete control of my life. Balance out my prayer. Take me deeper in my walk with you so I can move from petition to presence. Lord, I just want to be in your presence. I just want to sit at your feet. I declare and decree that I am responsible. I declare and decree that I will show up decently and in order. I declare and decree that every issue and every matter will be repaired, restored, and resolved in Jesus' name. Thank you, God. Amen.

In the same way, faith by itself, if it is not accompanied by action, is dead. – James 2:17

His divine power has granted to us all things that pertain to life and godliness, through the knowledge of him who called us to his own glory and excellence, – 2 Peter 1:3

Do not be conformed to this world, but be transformed by the renewal of your mind, that by testing you may discern what is the will of God, what is good and acceptable and perfect. – Romans 12:2

Blessed is the man who remains steadfast under trial, for when he has stood the test he will receive the crown of life, which God has promised to those who love him. – James 1:12

For at one time you were darkness, but now you are light in the Lord. Walk as children of light – Ephesians 5:8

25

A prayer on
how to pray

> *"Do not be anxious about anything, but in everything by prayer and supplication with thanksgiving let your requests be made known to God."*
> **- Philippians 4:6**

I F YOU'RE IN A PLACE RIGHT NOW WHERE YOU ARE SEEKING, yearning, and wanting more of God, then let me just say: I salute you, my sister! Just when you get into the position of thirsting after the Lord, God will begin to move mountains in your life. As you turn your heart towards God, He is there already waiting for you. The way you get closer to God is similar to the way you get close to a man. You remember when you first met that person of interest? You liked him and you wanted to get to know him. Then perhaps, you wanted more of him? So you followed a progression from not knowing this person to wanting to know this person more intimately. Let's call this person "Bo." Well, our initial encounter to go deeper in our walk with the Lord is similar to our initial encounter with Bo. How we get to know Bo and establish a meaningful relationship is dependent upon how often we spend time with Bo. And in our quality time with Bo, we talk and we listen. We have scheduled dates that are priority over and above anything else. We share things that we wouldn't share with any other person; you know, things like our hopes and dreams, our feelings and frustrations. At some point in time down the road, we learn that we have established a deep connection with Bo as a result of us spending concentrated time with him. In the same way, we are to spend time with God until our relationship over time grows into a strong connection. That is how we come to know God better and more deeply.

So the task at hand my sister friend, is time with God in prayer. If you don't know how to pray or if you're asking yourself the question, "How do I pray correctly," here's what you should know. There is no right way or wrong way to pray. Prayer is simply a conversation with God. Remember, he is our father in heaven. He loves us. So, in the same way you might have a conversation with your earthly father, who loves you and adores you, this is how you should have a conversation with your Heavenly Father. There is a model prayer that you may be familiar with:

After this manner therefore pray ye: Our Father which art in heaven, Hallowed be thy name. Thy kingdom come, Thy will be done in earth, as it is in heaven. Give us this day our daily bread. And forgive us our debts, as we forgive our debtors. And lead us not into temptation, but deliver us from evil: For thine is the kingdom, and the power, and the glory, forever. Amen. – Matthew 6:9-13 King James Version (KJV)

This is a model prayer. This is the response that Jesus gives the disciples when they ask him to teach them how to pray. So you can pray this prayer or use it as a model for the contents of your prayer when you do pray. Most importantly, always acknowledge God in the beginning of your prayer. You can acknowledge God in many different ways. When you lift up his name, you are essentially lifting up the name of God in adoration and acknowledgment. Then, make sure you are welcoming the power of God, which is the Holy Spirit. Think about it…. If you're asking God for divine intervention, or if you are believing God to do the unimaginable, then you need the power of God. Therefore, you must welcome the Holy Spirit into your prayer in order to access that same power which rose Jesus Christ from the dead. Next, we must offer a personal confession when we go before the Lord to signify that you believe in Jesus the Christ as Lord. He was raised from the dead and sent to pay for our sins. Moving any obstacles that might be in the way of you and "Dad" is necessary in prayer. In fact, if you feel like there is a block in your connection with God, consider that unforgiveness is a major block. The Word of the Lord says, "And when you stand praying, if you hold anything against anyone, forgive them, so that your Father in heaven may forgive you your sins." Certainly acknowledging all that God is in all that God does, is a prayer in and of itself. Think about how would you feel when you have done something for someone else and they continue to come to you without acknowledging what you've done. So make up in your mind in whatever way you come to God (whether formally or casually), that you always give God his due. In other words, always express your gratitude. These are the very basic fundamentals that we learn from a model prayer.

Here are some other things that are critical to you if you want to grow deeper in your spiritual walk with God. Matthew 6:33 says, "Seek first the kingdom of God," which is a command of God to make him a priority. It is important that you come to God first on all things. Going to God should be the first thing you do when you wake up in the morning. You must literally put God before everything else. You should also go to God first for every matter that shows up in life. That is what it means to seek Him first. Your prayer time in the morning is considered planned pro-active prayer. That means, you are praying before things happen so that God can equip *when* things happen. Because trust me, things are bound to happen. Thus, when you take God serious-ly enough to make Him priority, and when you pray in advance before adversity strikes, you earn the right for God to turn his ear to you whenever you call on him. Wouldn't you feel better knowing that you have graduated from seeking God just when you need something? Prioritizing God and praying proactively should be your goal as a believer. This will help you to have a healthy and balanced life with the Lord. Never let anyone interfere with your scheduled time with God. In fact, treat your time with God like a date night with Bo. When you really want to spend time with someone you care about, you will not let anything else interfere with that scheduled time slot. In the same way, that is exactly the posture you must take on with God if you want to grow deeper in your walk.

1. Guard and protect your prayer time with the Lord
2. Pray the names of God
3. Pray in the Scriptures
4. Use the model prayer for content/format
5. Pray with a sincere heart even if you don't know the right words (Hebrews 10:22)
6. Have a conversation with God (Matthew 6:7)
7. Keep a list of what's on your heart and what areas you are believing God to show up
8. Be obedient to the prayer (Luke 6:46)
9. Seal your prayer "in Jesus' name" (john 14:13)
10. Pray in faith (mark 11:24)

These are just some things to consider when you are praying. In addition, you are also to pray about praying. Let Dad know that you want more of Him in your life and you are seeking a deeper relationship with Him. Talk about the problem, not the answer. Approach the throne of grace boldly according to the Word, believing that you have anything that you ask according to God's will. Have faith when you pray, because doubt will cancel faith.

I come to you Abba Father
(Romans 8:15)

Father, in the name of Jesus, I come to you right now thanking you for being God. I thank you for the privilege of being called your daughter. I'm grateful for our relationship Father; that you accepted me before I turned to you. Now, in my very simple language, I love you. I love you, Dad. Help me to learn how to pray. Help me to learn how to cover myself in prayer. Teach me how to just be in your presence and not to always petition you. I declare and decree that I have graduated from random prayer that is based on the events of my life and I now ask you to take me higher. Help me to develop my prayer language, to be comfortable coming to you and confident in you. Show me who I need to pray for and how. I declare and decree that your words shall fill my mouth and my heart that I might be effective in prayer. I believe the Spirit will help me in my weakness when I do not know what I ought to pray for, because the Spirit Himself intercedes for me through wordless groans (Romans 8:26.) Thank you for hearing my heart. I surrender this prayer to you, in Jesus' name, Amen.

If you abide in me, and my words abide in you, ask whatever you wish, and it will be done for you. – John 15:7

Do not be anxious about anything, but in everything by prayer and supplication with thanksgiving let your requests be made known to God. – Philippians 4:6

Therefore I tell you, whatever you ask in prayer, believe that you have received it, and it will be yours. – Mark 11:24

And when you pray, do not heap up empty phrases as the Gentiles do, for they think that they will be heard for their many words. – Matthew 6:7

And I tell you, ask, and it will be given to you; seek, and you will find; knock, and it will be opened to you. – Luke 11:9

26

A prayer when your prayers aren't being answered

> *"But your iniquities have made a separation between you and your God, and your sins have hidden his face from you so that he does not hear."*
> **– Isaiah 59:2 / 28 helpful votes**

I N MY MANY YEARS WORKING IN CORPORATE AMERICA, I learned a lot of valuable lessons on life and leadership. Many of those lessons, I now know, are rooted in biblical principles. And when the things you learn in the natural are supported by spiritual principles, it makes applying that lesson so much easier. One lesson I learned in Corporate was a method called the Johari window. This model is a four quadrant tool intended to clarify what we know about ourselves versus what we don't know. It is typically used for personal growth and development. Its primary goal is to help a leader see his/her blind spots. That way, if someone can see his or her blind spots, then they no longer live their lives in the dark. There is nothing hidden, and they have clarity on where they are so they can reach their intended destination.

So why am I sharing this with you? In my ministry women are my primary target and using prayer as a primary tool over time I've come across one common prayer. That prayer is "What am I missing?" A conversation about this usually sounds like: "why won't God answer my prayer? It seems my prayers aren't getting through..." In a lot of instances, women will share how long they've been waiting for God to answer them, as if to say, "God should've shown up by now." Then, I get the question (which I think is an excellent question to ask)... "What am I missing?" Whenever you ask a question to the God of the universe, the answer will somehow be given. So if you ask better questions, then I believe you'll get better answers. When this very question came from a woman one day in a moment of despair, she got her answer.

This scenario may resonate with you as well. You're a good woman. You would be willing to work. You take care of yourself and your responsibilities. You love God and you do the best that you can with what you have. But you can't seem to get a break and you desperately need a breakthrough. You desperately want to know "what am I missing?"

If this is your situation? Here's what I have learned is a major miss for so many women. Even though you are doing fairly well in life, and even though you love God, is it possible that you are doing the bare minimum and not following God fully? In other words, does your faith walk only consist of church and maybe prayer, but you miss many of the very obvious fundamentals required by God?

An example of what it means to not follow God fully, is the case of the children of Israel. God brought the Israelites out of Egypt. He delivered them from bondage. But they came to a divide in the road. God promised he was going to bring the children of Israel to the land of Canaan, but they did not accept the offer to follow God all the way. As a result, they were not able to partake in the full abundance of God. Could it be that you trust

God to save you, free you from sin and to get you into heaven, however you don't follow God completely? It's like you live in the home with your father who provides covering and protection, but you don't have access to all that he has for you because you don't follow his rules. Well that's how it is in the kingdom if you don't obey the commands of God. God will keep you because He loves you. However Joshua tells the story of how you are blessed above measure when you are obedient. There's a difference between being the daughter who is kept and the daughter who is blessed. The children who were kept wandering in the wilderness for 40 years. The children who were blessed were those who entered the Promised Land because of their full obedience.

Here are some examples of the disobedience that may be blocking your breakthrough.

Are you praying for a financial breakthrough, however you fail to give God what He asks of you?

Are you praying for a job or a promotion, however you neglect, disrespect and disregard your current employer?

Are you asking God for a better and bigger house/car, yet you don't take care of what you currently have?

Are you believing God for a husband or a yummy relationship, however you disrespected, neglected, lied or cheated on someone else in a previous relationship; and you have not reconciled with God?

Are you diligent in your prayer life but struggle with gossip, spewing hate and talking about other people?

These are just examples of how we block our blessings when we pray in one direction and we dishonor God in another. So, if your prayers are not being answered, consider what you're asking of God and what He's asking of you in that same area. Sure we know God's ways are not our ways, but His way has a traceable pattern. God promises to bless those who walk in full obedience (Deuteronomy 28:1-14.) If your prayers are not being answered, is disobedience a block? If your prayers are not being answered, are you mismanaging what you currently have?

Greatness, let me drop this in your spirit. If God has not answered your prayers, it doesn't mean He doesn't love you. If God has not delivered on your prayers, it does not mean He can't. "Look at the birds of the air; they do not sow or reap or store away in barns, and yet your heavenly Father feeds them. Are you not much more valuable than they?" (Matthew 6:26) If God has not shown Himself to you, maybe it is just a matter of time before He will intervene. If He hasn't come, you still have hope as a believer that He will. The Word of the Lord says in Jeremiah 29:11, "For I know the plans that I have for you declares the Lord plans not to harm you but plans to prosper you, to give you hope and a future." If God has not answered your prayer yet, accept that it may be a temporary roadblock intended to teach you what you most need to know in order for you to go deeper in your walk with the Lord.

I come to you God of Hope
(Titus 2:13)

Father God, in the name of Jesus, I come to you to give your name all the praise and glory. I come to you declaring that you are the head of my life. I come to you to present my heart. Lord, I've been praying for sometime about so many thing, and I have yet to hear from you. But now God I realize that I may be in my own way. I recognize Lord when I petition you and then I don't hear from you, that I may be unrealistic in my expectations and out of order in my spiritual walk. So Lord, will you please forgive me? Forgive me of my sins of omission and commission. Forgive me for not being a good steward over all that you have placed in my hands.

Now Dad, would you help me to be responsible? Help me Lord to show up decently and in order in all areas of my life. Lord, I know that I own nothing and I am nothing without you. "The earth is the LORD's, and everything in it, the world, and all who live in it." (Psalm 24:1.)" Lord help me to live according to Your Word in Luke 16:10; and to be faithful in the little things. I declare and decree that I am responsible. I declare and decree that I am no longer just a hearer of the Word, but a doer of the Word as well. Lord, move me out of my own way and have your way in my life. Let me walk like a woman of integrity and do what I need to do to honor you. However you choose to bless me, I will be satisfied...in Jesus' name, I pray...Amen.

You ask and do not receive, because you ask wrongly, to spend it on your passions. – James 4:3

And whatever you ask in prayer, you will receive, if you have faith. – Matthew 21:22

Ask, and it will be given to you; seek, and you will find; knock, and it will be opened to you. – Matthew 7:7

But let him ask in faith, with no doubting, for the one who doubts is like a wave of the sea that is driven and tossed by the wind. – James 1:6

And this is the confidence that we have toward him, that if we ask anything according to his will he hears us. – 1 John 5:14

27

A prayer when you are going through a storm

> *"When you pass through the waters, I will be with you; and when you pass through the rivers, they will not sweep over you. When you walk through the fire, you will not be burned; the flames will not set you ablaze."*
> **– Isaiah 43:2**

I F YOU ARE IN THE STORM OF YOUR LIFE AND YOU FEEL LIKE you are drowning and there is no indication that you are coming out of this, please hold on and don't give up. At least until you finish this chapter. The storms that we endure in life are no surprise to God. In fact God tells us that we will endure storms but He will be with us. "When you pass through the waters, I will be with you and when you pass through the rivers, they will not sweep over you. When you walk through the fire, you will not be burned. The flames will not set you ablaze" (Isaiah 43:2.) The mere fact that God will be with us is an indication that the storm is part of his divine plan. I'm sure you may not want to hear this but the storm in your life is purposeful. It will not be wasted. It will produce a result in alignment with what God is doing in your life.

The bigger problem when Christians go through a rocky spot or a wilderness season, is that we act surprised and then we lose hope. How do we resolve this? First, remember that God is our insulation. That means, He will keep us through the storm so that we will be protected. God never promised isolation from trials. "In this world, you will have trouble. But take heart because I have overcome the world" (John 16:33.) God will even tell us that a storm is coming so we will know what to expect in life and be at peace trusting Him. You must resist looking at your storm and falling into a hole of hopelessness. Whatever your issue, it may feel overwhelming, all consuming, larger than life, or a nail in your coffin, but the truth of the matter is, it's not bigger than God. God is bigger, greater, and more powerful than anything you are going through. God is able to do the impossible in any and every situation. Your situation is not new to God and it's not anything that He hasn't already overcome. You just have to line up your faith with God's Word on the matter and He will bring you out of the storm. He will allow you to outrun the enemy who is trying his best to wear you out.

Your job is to call it how you see it. If you're in a storm, be clear about whether this is a category one, two, or three type storm. Then you will know how to respond. Remember God plan for your life is to give you hope and a future. His plan is not to harm you. (Jeremiah 29:11.) So as long as you are living, then you have hope. In fact, the hallmark of a believer is that we have hope in Christ. Once you receive that word, then you will be able to re-sist the enemy's attempt to convince you that he is winning when in fact God has already won the victory. When you stay focused and clear that God is with you, then you can train your brain to look for the lesson in the storm and the greater purpose beyond the storm. Lastly, practice your victory two-step in advance. No matter how strong the winds may blow, the good news is, you are going to come out of it! But the only way to come out of your storm...is to walk through it.

I come to you God my Refuge
(Jeremiah 16:19)

Father God in the name of Jesus, I come before you right now with a broken spirit. Lord, you know my situation and you know my struggle. I feel like the cords of death have me bound. I'm believing you to lend me your ear. Please, Lord, save me. "You are the Lord who is kind and you do what is right. You are merciful." Your Word says, "You watch over the foolish and when I am helpless you are the one to save me." (Psalm 116 NCV.) I believe it and I receive that word, oh God. I'm not trusting in flesh, God; I'm putting everything on you. Nothing is too hard for you. You specialize in impossible situations. Please come and see about my impossible situation. I'm trusting you, Emmanuel. I believe you are with me. Now God, stay with me. Hold my hand and allow me to feel your presence. Remove the weight of my struggle, Lord, and help me to rest at night. Reduce my stress and worry. Thank you for grace and mercy. Please, would you give me discernment and patience to walk through this? I praise you in advance for the victory. In Jesus' name, I pray amen.

And when he got into the boat, his disciples followed him. And behold, there arose a great storm on the sea, so that the boat was being swamped by the waves; but he was asleep. And they went and woke him, saying, "Save us, Lord; we are perishing." And he said to them, "Why are you afraid, O you of little faith?" Then he rose and rebuked the winds and the sea, and there was a great calm. And the men marveled, saying, "What sort of man is this, that even winds and sea obey him?" – Matthew 8:23-27

Be strong and courageous. Do not fear or be in dread of them, for it is the Lord your God who goes with you. He will not leave you or forsake you." – Deuteronomy 31:6

He made the storm be still, and the waves of the sea were hushed. – Psalm 107:29

When the righteous cry for help, the Lord hears and delivers them out of all their troubles. The Lord is near to the brokenhearted and saves the crushed in spirit. Many are the afflictions of the righteous, but the Lord delivers him out of them all. He keeps all his bones; not one of them is broken. – Psalm 34:17-20 / 87 helpful votes

The Lord is good, a stronghold in the day of trouble; he knows those who take refuge in him. – Nahum 1:7

28
A prayer when you are overcome with "holiday" grief

> *"Blessed are those who mourn,*
> *for they shall be comforted."*
> *– Matthew 5:4*

I'LL NEVER FORGET GETTING A TEXT MESSAGE THAT BROUGHT me to tears. It read, "I just want Christmas to be over. I can't wait until January 1." Turns out, the message was from a friend who had lost her mother to illness a year prior. Christmas had become a very difficult time for her. Christmas is the time of year when families get together. And "happy" is the predetermined norm for most Americans who are Christian. The problem with that is, if Christmas is a reminder of a difficult time for you, then just living in that season can be challenging. Sweet little baby Jesus is overshadowed by your pain; and if you are broke, broken, hurt and struggling, then you just want the season to pass as quickly as possible. Furthermore, while Christmas should be a time to celebrate the birth of Christ, both commercialism and consumerism, from "Black Friday" into New Years, tend to upstage Jesus' birthday.

When I received that text from my friend, I did what I believed was the only thing I could do as a bystander. I told her I would pray for her. I knew there was nothing else I could say or do that would comfort her or make the pain go away. Because this is your situation, no one will ever understand your pain, even if they have been through something similar. Even if they have lost a parent, grieving is not the same for any two people. It's okay for you to grieve for however long you need to. There is no book or rules for grieving, just God's Word: "blessed be the God and Father of our Lord Jesus Christ, the Father of mercies and the God of comfort who comforts us in all our affliction..." (2 Corinthians 1:3.) It's okay to not conform to the ways of the world during the holiday. It's okay to be independent in your thinking during the Christmas holiday. It's okay for you to go against the grain and be opposite of everyone else during the season.

As I said, there's nothing that anyone can do for you but there is something that you can do for yourself. Remember Christ in this season. Never forget Him nor give up on Him. Trust God to decrease your pain and suffering over time. Trust God to move you from tolerance to acceptance one day. Trust God to give you creative and divine inspiration to celebrate your loved ones in a new way that will ultimately bring you peace. Then, create proactive plans to vacate during the holidays or to do something that will acknowledge God as Lord and honor the memory of your loss.

I come to you God my Rock
(1 Corinthians 10:4)

Father God in the name of Jesus, I come to you with a heavy heart. You know the pain of my cries, the story of my tears, the hole in my heart, and the loss of an appetite to celebrate during Christmas and other family gatherings. Now God, help me to resolve this today. Lord, I want to feel better. I know death is in your plan and I am a true believer in eternal life. But it doesn't make losing [mom/dad/child/sibling *name*] any easier. Lord, would you protect me from awkward situations and conversations with family and friends who are only trying to help? Speak to them on my behalf, God, or speak through me so I might have the words to share and they will receive it. Give me the strength to manage obligations during this season, or make a way of escape. Help me not to be a killjoy for my family in this season. Give others understanding and speak to them about giving me space to grieve with no judgment or unsolicited advice. Lord, if there is a resource that I need, please show me and make it plain. I resist every attempt of the enemy to dispatch a cloud of depression over me. Lord, I know you're going to bring me through this with time, but if it is your will to perform a miracle in my life so that this death grip would move itself from me, do it. I receive it. In Jesus' name, I pray amen.

Come to me, all who labor and are heavy laden, and I will give you rest. Take my yoke upon you, and learn from me, for I am gentle and lowly in heart, and you will find rest for your souls. For my yoke is easy, and my burden is light." – Matthew 11:28-30

Blessed be the God and Father of our Lord Jesus Christ, the Father of mercies and God of all comfort, who comforts us in all our affliction, so that we may be able to comfort those who are in any affliction, with the comfort with which we ourselves are comforted by God. – 2 Corinthians 1:3-4

Blessed are those who mourn, for they shall be comforted. – Matthew 5:4

He heals the brokenhearted and binds up their wounds. – Psalm 147:3

He will wipe away every tear from their eyes, and death shall be no more, neither shall there be mourning, nor crying, nor pain anymore, for the former things have passed away." – Revelation 21:4

29

A prayer when your marriage is on the rocks

> 'Ah, Lord God! It is you who have made the
> heavens and the earth by your great power and
> by your outstretched arm! Nothing is too hard for you.'
> – **Jeremiah 32:17**

BEING MARRIED CAN BE CHALLENGING. THAT PRETTY MUCH goes without saying. For the happily married couples reading this, God bless you. For the painfully struggling couples, may God help you. I believe God is for marriage, but the truth of the matter is, more than 50% of marriages end in divorce. And that statistic is even higher, unfortunately, for married believers. The reason there are so many divorces in the church is because we don't know what to do. We don't know how to handle crisis. We don't know how to resolve our issues. We have never been taught *how* to be a wife.

It used to really bother me that we live in a world where formal education (which prepares you for a career), and career skills are valued more than life skills. Because we place greater emphasis on spending 12+ years educating ourselves for a job, it's no surprise that the divorce rate is so high. It's because we have never been taught these critical life skills like how to be a parent, how to be a wife, how to manage grief and how to manage your money. So in an attempt to share the Cliff Notes for how to course-correct what had never been taught to you, here's how you can begin to resolve your marriage if you are in trouble.

Communication is one of the top three reasons people divorce. Although communication is more than time spent talking, we have a tendency to talk too much as women. In fact, research shows that women use approximately 20,000 words per day and men use only 7,000. Talking too much and not praying enough is our first-issue. Start praying about your marriage and develop the habit of talking to God about your husband *before* you talk *to* your husband. If you use that formula, God can manage your tongue. The Word of the Lord says death and life are in the power of the tongue. Truth of the matter is, some women speak death and destruction and divorce over their marriage. They sow seeds of negativity to their husbands, and what they don't understand is, what you put out is what you will bring back. Therefore, pray to God that He will show you your role and responsibility, not just your husband's flaws. Ask God to allow you to be the wife God wants you to be for your husband. Ask God to make your husband into who He wants him to be, rather than begging God to change him according to your desires. Once you have shifted your prayer language to cover your husband, seek professional help from a licensed trained therapist. This person may not necessarily be your pastor, unless he or she is a licensed and trained in therapy. It is okay to have a relationship covering, but that is not a substitute for professionally trained resources. You should seek both. Men often struggle with sharing their issues in a professional setting like counseling. So consider other creative ways for divine intervention. The third and often best support that you can have when you're struggling in your marriage is a loving married couple as your best friends. If they are believers (not churchy) and they are strong in their walk and committed to their marriage, then they will serve as positive role models for you. And prayerfully, your husband may find a confidant who will hold him accountable.

I come to you God my Mediator
(1 Timothy 2:5)

Father, in the name of Jesus, I come before you God. You know my struggle and you know the pain I feel about the covenant that I took before you. Lord, I don't know what to do. I believe you are for marriage and I took my vows seriously. I may not have done this perfectly, God, but I know you are a forgiving God. You are a merciful God. Forgive me for whatever I have done that was not pleasing in your sight. Now God, would you please come and see about my marriage? Would you come and see about my husband, oh God? You know the struggle; you know the issue; you know the need; you know the situation and the circumstance. I lift this *[names issue]* to you because your Word says so. Lord, would you make this word a reality in our hearts. In Galatians 5, you command us to be gentle, faithful, patient, loving and women of self-control. Enable me to get there again. Help me to love according to your word in 1 Corinthians 13:7. Release me, God, from being rude or disrespectful, irritable or resentful to my husband when I do not get my own way. Give me the ability to forgive as you have forgiven me. Help me, Lord to bear all things, believe all things, endure all things and to hope in all things; especially in the wonderful possibilities of our future. I leave you with this God because you are the God of the impossible. I surrender to you, and submit to my husband. Have your way. Move me out of your way. In Jesus' name. Amen.

But the fruit of the Spirit is love, joy, peace, patience, kindness, goodness, faithfulness, gentleness, self-control; against such things there is no law. – Galatians 5:22-23

For this very reason, make every effort to supplement your faith with virtue, and virtue with knowledge, and knowledge with self-control, and self-control with steadfastness, and steadfastness with godliness, and godliness with brotherly affection, and brotherly affection with love. – 2 Peter 1:5-7

Be kind to one another, tenderhearted, forgiving one another, as God in Christ forgave you. – Ephesians 4:32

Love is patient and kind; love does not envy or boast; it is not arrogant or rude. It does not insist on its own way; it is not irritable or resentful; it does not rejoice at wrongdoing, but rejoices with the truth. Love bears all things, believes all things, hopes all things, and endures all things. – 1 Corinthians 13:4-7

Wives, submit to your own husbands, as to the Lord. For the husband is the head of the wife even as Christ is the head of the church, His body, and is Himself its Savior. Now as the church submits to Christ, so also wives should submit in everything to their husbands, – Ephesians 5:22-33

30
A prayer for those who have little faith

"For we walk by faith, not by sight."
– 2 Corinthians 5:7

THE WORD SAYS, "HOW CAN YOU SAY YOU LOVE GOD BUT you do not do what I say." Obedience is the evidence that you love and have faith in God. Without "doing" the Word of God, your faith is in question. Too many people say they have faith in God yet they do not follow the Word.

For a little while, there was a running joke with my mother who is a legendary make-up artist, very witty and comical, but a woman of God nonetheless. The joke was that she would always say, "I need to see it in order to believe it. I need to see it in order to have faith." We would laugh because I knew that wasn't faith at all. In fact, it's quite the opposite. Faith is believing in what you can't see. Faith is action and effort in what you cannot see with your natural eye. For my mother, as much as I know my mother loves the Lord, without question, she was also a skeptic and she had to see it in order to believe it. So, my mom is a classic case of how someone can love God based on their own definition of God, until they learn otherwise. Good thing for her is that God really matured her in her faith walk and now, she has evidence of her belief, faith and love for God.

If you have struggled with trusting God beyond what you can see in front of you, or if you have ever dealt with the conflict of loving God but not believing in God, let me drop this in your spirit. Faith is the substance of what you hope for when you have no evidence in front of you. You may believe and feel that you love God with all your heart. The truth is, however, if you are the one who believes only if you can see it, then you love God based on your reference of love and not based on God's definition of love. To increase your faith and to grow in your spiritual walk, you must learn, receive and accept God's prerequisites. In order to come to God, you must first believe in Him. Where we often show up lacking is when we ask God to bless us but we don't believe in Him for all things. This showed up recently when I encountered three women in route to T.D Jakes' annual "Woman Thou Art Loosed" conference. One of the women was still in bondage and afraid to get on an elevator. I said to her, "are you believing God for some things in your life"? Of course she said, "Yes." My next question, then, was "How is it that you can believe God to bless you but you won't believe God to resolve your fear?" I shared with her that I believed her blessing was just outside of her comfort zone, on the downside of the escalator. I use that as a metaphor to say, fear and faith can't reside in the same place. You cannot be a woman of faith and have fear at the same time. It doesn't make sense. You are an ambassador of Christ. You're here to represent God and your best representation would be to walk out your faith fully and not allow the enemy to label you as a faux Christian. The only measure of faith is action to demonstrate your faith. Otherwise you can continue to say what you believe, but until you have an experiential opportunity to exercise your faith, then you will have no evidence to prove to yourself.

I come to you Living Water
(John 4:10)

Father, in the name of Jesus, I come before you right now. I love you and there's no doubt in my mind. However, I now realize that my knowledge of the Word and Your commands are limited. Since there is so much that I may not know about the Word at a deeper level, I'm asking you today to increase my knowledge of your Word. Help me to not just be a listener or a hearer of the Word, but to be a doer of Your Word. (James 1:22) I receive this question as a charge to step up into complete alignment "Why do you call me, 'Lord, Lord,' and do not do what I say?" (Like 6:46.) I resist the enemy's invitation to keep me small and surface level. Increase my faith and action. Help me prove myself in deep. In Jesus' name, I pray, Amen.

So faith comes from hearing, and hearing through the word of Christ. – Romans 10:17

And without faith it is impossible to please him, for whoever would draw near to God must believe that he exists and that he rewards those who seek him. – Hebrews 11:6

Now faith is the assurance of things hoped for, the conviction of things not seen. – Hebrews 11:1

For we walk by faith, not by sight. – 2 Corinthians 5:7

But be doers of the word, and not hearers only, deceiving yourselves. – James 1:22

31

A prayer for God to change your attitude

> "What you have learned and received and
> heard and seen in me—practice these things,
> and the God of peace will be with you."
> - **Philippians 4:9**

W HEN I WAS A LITTLE GIRL, I REMEMBER MY MOTHER and maybe others saying to me: *you have an attitude.* Now, when I got older, of course I understood that everyone has an attitude…so, yes, I have an attitude. But back then, what that meant for a little brown girl like me, was to say, "Girl, you have a bad attitude or a negative attitude." It may have even meant that I was sassy. What I didn't understand back then was the power of an attitude and how it could impact one's life. My mother probably called me out because she felt my energy and she knew it wasn't a good look for a little girl to walk around with an attitude.

So the lesson I learned and that people both young and old need to know is this: your attitude will determine your altitude. Just as my mother might've been annoyed that the little brown girl in me had an attitude and she didn't want to be around me, a positive attitude will do just the opposite. The way that your attitude works is simple. Like energy, it attracts back what you put out. If you are negative, then you will attract negative energy. If you are positive, then you are more likely to attract positive energy. Positive people are a joy to be around. When people like you, better options, opportunities and positions will flood your life. The more options you have and the more access you have in the world, will lead to a better quality of life. Be clear: there is a positive correlation between your attitude and your altitude. If you can't be positive and get along with other people, then every area of your life will be affected. Your job opportunities, your relationships with coworkers and even your relationship with family members will all be affected.

I once worked with someone who had a funky attitude, and as a result, I called off all deals with them. In another instance, I met someone at a conference whose energy and attitude was at 100 and decided I was going to find a way to work with that individual. I have seen instances where people will bend over backwards for people based on one's attitude.

Because we are human creatures of choice, wired in such a way that our emotions are not automatic but reactionary, then consider this, greatness: there may be situations that contribute to how you show up in life. If you struggle with having an attitude, you most certainly need to pray and ask God to fix it quickly. If you find yourself not keeping a job, not keeping a man, not keeping good friends and deflecting good people from your life, then maybe it's an attitude problem that is affecting your altitude.

God has already spoken on the issue of attitude. You are an ambassador of Christ. Therefore in order to represent God, you've got to show up with some resemblance that you are a Kingdom citizen. You are a believer and commanded to follow the standard; that is to be happy and delight yourself in the Lord. Even if circumstances confirm that you have every reason to be negative about life, the Word of the Lord says that you can control your emotions. So begin today by praying for God to change your attitude, so that you can ultimately change your altitude.

I come to you Light of the World
(John 8:12)

Father, in the name of Jesus, I come before you to honor and praise to your name. Thank you for creating me, a mere image and mortal being. Because you made me like you, Lord, would you please perfect me in the area of my demeanor, energy, attitude and disposition? I lay my harsh, rigid, vocal, aggressive and negative attitude before you. I ask you to get me together, Lord. I want to be more like you. I want to be the woman you called me to be. Lord, help me to process whatever unresolved issues are buried so that I can reconcile and then rediscover who I need to be for you. Forgive me for any relationship where I have been at fault. Help me to have an open heart and mind, and to show up decently and in order God. Make my spirit sweet and my personality likable so that I might be used by you Lord to do good work. Lord, use me to make a good presentation for you as I walk this walk. I resist any attempt from the enemy to keep me in a negative attitude. I welcome new people who think differently and I willingly embrace positivity. I surrender this prayer in Jesus' name, Amen.

Do all things without grumbling or questioning, that you may be blameless and innocent, children of God without blemish in the midst of a crooked and twisted generation, among whom you shine as lights in the world, – Philippians 2:14-15

Finally, brothers, whatever is true, whatever is honorable, whatever is just, whatever is pure, whatever is lovely, whatever is commendable, if there is any excellence, if there is anything worthy of praise, think about these things. – Philippians 4:8

Whatever you do, work heartily, as for the Lord and not for men. – Colossians 3:23

And have put on the new self, which is being renewed in knowledge after the image of its creator. – Colossians 3:10

A joyful heart is good medicine, but a crushed spirit dries up the bones. – Proverbs 17:22

32
A prayer when your identity is in question

> *"Before I formed you in the womb I knew you, a*
> *nd before you were born I consecrated you;*
> *I appointed you a prophet to the nations."*
> **– Jeremiah 1:5**

*Y*OU'RE FIRED. YUP. IT'S HAPPENED TO ME, TOO. THE FIRST time it happened, it was one of my best life lessons. I was a young professional working for a Fortune 100 company. The corporate office was restructuring and my department was one of many who had a massive wave of eliminating jobs. So technically I was not fired, but, in my opinion, d*ownsizing, right sizing, layoff or firing... it's all the same.* There's no need to use comfortable language to save face. If you didn't leave by choice, you were fired. If you leaving was not an option and certain things happened beyond your control, you were fired. . But even in this, I believe my separation from that corporate job was a strategic God-move in my life.

Here I was, walking out of the big corporate campus (that resembled a plush country club from the outside) with all my belongings in one brown box. My boss offered to walk me out to my car. We said our goodbyes and I was home within 15 minutes. It was finished… and there I was wondering, "What now"? I had never been without a job; so for the first time in my early moments of introspection, I realized that all of my adult life I was identified by an employer. I was attached to work, the industry, and the prestige and of course the sense of accomplishment that came with being an employee of a "big brand industry leader." So the season that followed my termination presented me with a new question: "who are you?"

When you step into an awareness of who you are, the walls will come down and the floodgates will open. In order to do so, you must first let go of who you are not so you can grab hold of who God created you to be. Let go of what you are not so you can discover your authentic self. As sharp as you are with all your material possessions you are not your shoes, your handbag, your wardrobe or the wealthy designer whose name is attached. You are not your car, house, zip code, job, associations or affiliations. You are not what you do or what happened to you. You are not your issue or your temporary circumstance. You are not JUST a daughter, a mom, a wife/partner. You have an identity separate and apart from your possessions, roles and responsibilities.

If you tend to over-identify with being a wife or a mom or the leader of this and a member of that, ask God to release you. Certainly it's not going to happen overnight but you need to ask God now. You are here on purpose, for a purpose. God created you, your life plan and the thumbprint that gives you unique value. You are fearfully and wonderfully. Your worth is assessed by God no matter what season you are in or how much you have in your bank account. Your appraisal comes from God no matter if you are with or without a job. Your value is immeasurable whether you have a GED, a Ph.D. or no letters behind your name. Your significance in the earth is not subject to how you got here, how your mother and father connected or who raised you. Your identity flows from Your Father in heaven. The Word says the "the earth is the Lord's and everything in it." You belong to God. The Word says "let us make man in our image." God made you. The Word says "I knit you together in your mother's womb." God is the manufacturer; your parents were just the instrument He used and because He is the maker of all things, He wrote the instruction manual for your life. That instruction manual, the Word of God says "you are my workmanship created in Christ Jesus to do good work that He prepared in advance for you to do." But that's just the tip of the iceberg! The reason you must begin this process of transforming your mind about your identity NOW is to help you move to your authentic self. You need to be released from the grips of the enemy that is trying to keep you pre-occupied with the world. If he steals your identity, you won't know who you are, whose you are, who you were created to be and the call on your life. And when you are left in the dark about your real identity, you will not walk into your destiny. That is why I encourage you to pray without ceasing that God would reveal to you your true identity.

I come to you my Creator
(1 Peter 4:19)

Father, in the name of Jesus, I come before you to say thank you for divine insight on identity. I lay before you my desire to know who I am. I lay before you the mess below the surface of my insecurity. I lay before you my struggle with over identifying with people, places and things. I lay before you my attachment to roles [name it here] and responsibilities where it may be risky or even unhealthy. Lord, I am grateful the roles and responsibilities you have entrusted to me [daughter, sister, wife, mom, God mom, auntie, grand mom, friend, mentor etc.] and even the professional roles and associations [name it here], however help me to properly reassign those labels. God, my desire is to know who I am apart from everything external. Lord, help me to properly reposition those people, places, things, associations, affiliations and even my accomplishments or failures so I can accept your definition. Open my eyes and heart to begin this self-discovery journey so I can hear from you and receive whatever you say about me. Reveal my unique identity and make Your Word a reality in my heart so I no longer simply quote scripture, but I can also have a personal experience with Your Word. Lord, I trust you to resolve this issue of identity. In Jesus' name. Amen.

So God created man in his own image, in the image of God he created him; male and female he created them. – Genesis 1:27

Before I formed you in the womb I knew you, and before you were born I consecrated you; I appointed you a prophet to the nations. – Jeremiah 1:5

But you are a chosen race, a royal priesthood, a holy nation, a people for his own possession, that you may proclaim the Excellencies of him who called you out of darkness into his marvelous light. – 1 Peter 2:9

I have been crucified with Christ. It is no longer I who live, but Christ who lives in me. And the life I now live in the flesh I live by faith in the Son of God, who loved me and gave himself for me. – Galatians 2:20

In him we were also chosen, having been predestined according to the plan of him who works out everything in conformity with the purpose of his will. – Ephesians 1:11

33

A prayer for your boo/Boaz

> *"This is the confidence we have in approaching God: that if we ask anything according to his will, he hears us."*
> **- 1 John 5:14**

IT'S A SINGLE WOMAN'S DILEMMA. YOU ARE SINGLE AND YOU are waiting on your Boaz. You're waiting on your mister right and trying to hold out? Except you've been holding on for dear life and it doesn't feel like it's ever going to happen for you. I've been there. Single and saved with your heart set on marriage, babies and doing the right thing. You are waiting to meet the man of your dreams or trying to make something happen with the man right now but it feels like it's not going to happen for you. You keep attracting the wrong men. You either wind up with men who are crazy about you yet you have no interest, or you meet men whom you are not attracted to. The one you are interested in is not interested in you or he's not available. The only good relationship you have is complicated, messy or adulteress or, it is a live-in relationship "gone wrong." Or maybe you just don't meet men all. The bottom line is, you are single with a desire to be married and only God holds the plans for your yummy hubby. That is why you must pray about this, too.

A few years ago, in one of my coaching groups, a woman said, "I'll never get married, I'll never get married." I said, "Do you want to be married?" She replied yes. What she didn't realize was that she was cursing the very thing that she wanted. She was sending a mixed single. She was a woman of faith with no faith. She was a woman of faith but her walk was incongruent with her talk. She was actively working on her spiritual growth in the program but she had yet to learn her lessons. Lesson number one: life and death are in the power of the tongue, which means you have the power in your tongue to bless a thing or to curse a thing. Whatever you loose on earth will be loosed in heaven and whatever you bind on earth will be bound in heaven. In other words, what you speak out in the atmosphere is going to bring back to you whatever you speak. You Word will not return to you without producing a result.

One of the most powerful pieces of scripture is in Isaiah 55:11 "my words that come from my mouth are like rain and will produce the result. Whatever I want to accomplish will happen. Whatever I intend will come to pass." So the lesson in wanting a husband and speaking against it is simple: be careful not to curse the very possibility of your desires with casual reckless chatter sending mixed messages.

The second lesson is this: while I was waiting on my husband, God was waiting on me! Truth is wasn't ready to be married. I thought I was ready. Actually it was more like I wanted to be ready and had never considered if I was ready or not. So God revealed to me one day that I wasn't ready. I still had work to do on myself and that is another lesson. You don't attract in life what you want; you attract who you are. So if you desire to be married and you have a healthy, loving, quality, yummy relationship with the most wonderful man ever, you have to be that which you desire. Sometimes women have unrealistic expectations about what we want in men and it's mainly unrealistic because we, ourselves, are not able to offer what we asking for. My sister friend, you've got to work on you. Work on your spiritual growth and your personal development. Set a goal to be the best you that you can be and you will attract the best things for you. Don't get mad that you constantly attract average men if you yourself are average and not willing to do anything to better yourself.

The third lesson is to be ready when he comes and know how to receive him. Know what the Lord requires of you and then know how to massage his ego; know how to love him and learn how to be the soft landing pad for him. Know how to play to his sensitivity because the truth of the matter is, men are more sensitive than we are at times. Know how to appreciate him in his love language and not yours. Know how to discern when you have a real issue in the relationship vs. when you are subjecting him to your unresolved issues. Many ladies run men away when we have not done our work of putting God first. The word in Proverbs 31 speaks of a noble wife and gives us clear job description. So Greatness, line up your mouth with your heart. If it's your desire to be married and to have a yummy relationship, then trust and believe God for it. God loves you and it's His will to give you the desires of your heart. It doesn't matter how old you are, how many children you have, how messed up you think you are. It doesn't matter how many failed relationships you've had. It doesn't matter your situation or circumstance, God has wired us to be a helpmate so it is natural for us to want that. Be unapologetic about it. Hand it over to God and wait patiently for it. But in the meantime, work on you. Begin to speak into the universe your appreciation for your husband. Say it, speak it, believe it and receive it.

I come to you God my Maker
(Job 35:10)

Father, in the name of Jesus, help me Lord right now. I confess it is my desire to be in a loving committed relationship. Lord I know that you wrote the story of my life and you know all about me. I know you planted in me this desire so I bring it to you right now. Remove it or settle in my spirit with right intentions according to Your Will for my life. Lord, forgive me for whatever I have done to block my blessings. Forgive me for any irresponsible conduct, disloyalty, abuse or neglect that I have allowed or participated in up until this point. Forgive me for bringing my baggage into previous relationships and for expecting my ex to have no issues. Forgive me for having inappropriate expectations of my ex when I should have placed every expectation in you, Lord. Forgive me for neglecting my time with you the moment I meet a man. Forgive me for inappropriate mental weights (blaming myself or thinking of myself more highly than I ought.) Forgive me for the judgment I had in previous relationships and for the harsh words I used to tear him down. Help me to bring closure in my heart for every failed relationship. Help me to move forward. Correct my thinking so that it will line up with your thoughts of me. Fix my mouth to speak forth life into all people so when you send him, I will already know how to guide my tongue to line up with your standard. Give me direction so that I can become a better representation of you. Work it out according to your will. I surrender my desires and I believe you will send him in your time, not mine. In Jesus' Name. Amen

So also the tongue is a small member, yet it boasts of great things. How great a forest is set ablaze by such a small fire! – James 3:5

Whoever restrains his words has knowledge, and he who has a cool spirit is a man of understanding. – Proverbs 17:27

So is my word that goes out from my mouth: It will not return to me empty, but will accomplish what I desire and achieve the purpose for which I sent it. – Isaiah 55:11

Mary responded, "I am the Lord's servant. May everything you have said about me come true." And then the angel left her. – Luke 1:38

This is the confidence we have in approaching God: that if we ask anything according to his will, he hears us. – 1 John 5:14

34

A prayer for an ideal life

I WAS AT THE NAIL SALON RECENTLY AND A YOUNG VIETNAMESE woman named Chan was very curious about my work. She noticed that I was dressed for work, which was a rare occasion for me considering I'm usually in the nail shop pretty casual. Of course, being the overly enthusiastic extrovert that I am, I was more than willing to share with her. So I said, "I am en route to a client to conduct a training session on life skills." The conversation moved from one topic to another, until I found myself giving her a random coaching session in between basecoat, color, and topcoat. In that session I heard from Chan what I hear so often from women: "I don't know what I want. I don't know what I want to do." Those words indicate they haven't been taught and the teaching is a need for life skills. Life skills to help you learn how to live and how to win in life.

Now I could totally relate to Chan because not only had I heard this many times before from other women, but I remember being young and uncertain about what I wanted in life. So what did I do in my clueless days when there weren't any obvious option on a course to me the rules of the game? I did what most people do—I followed the natural progression of things. I followed the path of the universe and eventually God showed up to lead me in the right direction that would present many lessons in life.

Along the way, I learned that God had a predetermined plan for my life that I was unknown to me in details. I had no idea what was to come of my life. I had no dream or goals for myself or vision from God for quite some time. However over time with some intention to find answers I gained clarity and insight and eventually I aligned myself with the path that God had for me. That was the place where I found answers to the burning questions of life. I discovered who God created me to be and, what I wanted to do, where I wanted to go and I learned for my- self how true this statement is: God's plan is to prosper us and give us hope and a future.

Now I live my life 100% on purpose knowing what my purpose is and walking in the gift that God gave me. Once God helped me to sort through my life, He then gave me an assignment to help women like you to figure it out so that you, too, could step into the abundant life that God has for you.

If you, my sister friend, have asked yourself the same questions or you've had this dialogue in your head like Chan, let me drop this in your spirit. Your life matters. You matter. You are here by design. God created you and He has a plan for your life. Because He is the creator, your creator, He is the only one who holds the blueprint for your life. If you have questions about your life, look to God for the answers. If you were questioning why you live, why you breathe and what is your purpose here on earth, you must go to God and press Him on all sides for the answer. There is a positive correlation between you discovering your purpose and your relationship with God. If you want to know more about your life, then come closer to God. The distance you are from the answers is the same distance you are away from God. Even though your mother and your father may tell you a beautiful story about how you came to be or a not so pleasant tale of your humble beginnings, they are not responsible for your birth; God is. Whether you were a planned pregnancy or a special surprise delivery, God created you on purpose. Whether you were adopted, abandoned, or neglected as a child, God is the author and finisher of your life. He wrote the story. He knows your end from the beginning. He knows all about you.

So I say that to say, YOU matter. Your life matters. Your life has a high net worth on earth and in heaven. You have eternal value and a personal appraisal from the only source that matters, God. Because the Lord our Father wired us to be human creatures of choice, we have complete authorship over our lives and deciding what you want and then choosing the path. What you make of your life is up to you. But just remember: you were created in God's image and He wants the best for you!

Now that you have come into the knowledge of these truths, I declare to you now once you discover the master plan you will never need permission from any- one else to live your life. I declare to you now that you have every right to dream and imagine. I encourage you to dream outside of the box. Think about what you want outside of where you are right now. Think about how you want to live your life. Think about who you want to be. Think about what you want to have. Think about what you want to do. Think about where you want to go.

God will let you know if what you desire in the plan and therefore approved by Him. Your responsibility is to get quiet and to tune in to the desires of your heart. Remember, "If you believe, you will receive whatever you ask for in prayer." I press my faith with your faith and I believe God to move in your life.

I come to you Bread of Life
(John 6:35)

Father, in the name of Jesus, I thank you right now for the divine deposit. Lord, I was once in the dark and now the lights have been turned on. I confess, Lord, that I had not given much thought to what I wanted OR to what you wanted for me. Forgive me Lord for not knowing and allow me to forgive myself. God, would you now solidify in my spirit that you created me on purpose and for a purpose? Reveal and solidify in my spirit that you have a plan for my life, and then open my heart to receive and follow the path you have set before me. Draw me nearer to you, my sweet heavenly Father. Take me deeper into the knowledge of Christ and give me clarity. Move me out of my own way so I can tune in to the desires you have planted in me. Move people, places and things that are a distraction out of my life. Silence the incoming traffic. Move me from surface level Christianity, and help me to be a doer of the Word according to James 1:22. Take me higher and deeper. Order my steps according to Your Will that I may have a rich and rewarding life. In Jesus' name. Amen

For whoever would save his life will lose it, but whoever loses his life for my sake will find it. – Matthew 16:25

Jesus said to them, "I am the bread of life; whoever comes to me shall not hunger, and whoever believes in me shall never thirst. – John 6:35

For I know the plans I have for you, declares the Lord, plans for welfare and not for evil, to give you a future and a hope. – Jeremiah 29:11

The Lord will fulfill his purpose for me; your steadfast love, O Lord, endures forever. Do not forsake the work of your hands. – Psalm 138:8

For by him all things were created, in heaven and on earth, visible and invisible, whether thrones or dominions or rulers or authorities — all things were created through him and for him. – Colossians 1:16

35

A prayer about churchy Christians

"Let all bitterness and wrath and anger and clamor and
slander be put away from you, along with all malice.
Be kind to one another, tenderhearted, forgiving one
another, as God in Christ forgave you."
– Ephesians 4:31-32

I WILL NEVER FORGET A FEW DEFINING MOMENTS IN THE height of my spiritual walk with the Lord. One instance, I shed tears and another situation made me question my faith. They were all instances that were draining, hurtful, embarrassing and a bad example of what it means to be a Christian. One instance, while serving in church and after a long day of working, I walked into Bible study and was immediately pulled to the side by a Deaconess. There I stood exhausted, burnt out, overwhelmed from working in the church and all I wanted to do was to sit in the presence of God. I wanted to connect with God, so I showed up at Bible study expecting to be refueled, but I got sidetracked by a deaconess who wanted to talk to me about a "penny fundraiser." Out of respect, I sat down next to her and about 40 minutes later (yes 40 minutes), I walked down the long corridor towards the exit doors. I never made it to Bible study. I went home disappointed, weary, depleted and frustrated.

Another instance in my faith walk that really proves that there are evil people in the world, happened to me, yet again, while working in a church. I was running into the church sanctuary one day and an old female usher who had to be at least 100 years old slammed the door in my face. Now I over dramatize the situation (perhaps) because it was so unreal and it could have been scripted in a comedy. But there I was serving in a large church where I worked for the Senior Pastor, so she clearly knew my face. But she didn't care. She slammed the door and kept on moving. I thought it was hilarious. Me and this old lady were about to break out into a fight at the church... it definitely felt like a stage play called "Madea Goes to Church."

The last scenario was much more painful. I was a young woman working in the church when I saw one of the leaders acting out. She was an associate pastor who was not so nice, (some might even say she was evil, lazy and self-serving.) But during this encounter, she tried to flex her authority muscles and it became painful to watch. I remember going back into my office, shutting the door and crying. Later in a moment of strength, I thought to myself, "What a horrible witness." The quiet whisper over my shoulder said, "If I didn't know God already, I wouldn't want any part of the God she served." Luckily for me, I knew God at the time ...even though that was my first time witnessing firsthand the danger of misrepresentation.

All of that to say, here's what I know for sure. Whatever has happened in church to turn you away from the church, God has nevertheless called us to connect with the local body. So we can't run away from the church even if we have a personal relationship with Christ. The church is not for perfect people and there is no such thing as a perfect church. Jesus came for sinners, and we are all sinners saved by grace. The enemy tries to get in our head and use the imperfections of others and the shame of our faith walk to question God. Each situation I described was perhaps an intentional scheme of the enemy sent to throw me off course. His goal was to disconnect me from the local body of believers. When we are absent from the local body, we miss out on faith development. When you are absent from the local body, you miss the fellowship, you miss going deeper in the Word, and you miss growing in your relationship with God. And when you're absent from fellowship with God, you miss the opportunity to know your purpose in life. There are many things you miss when you are outside of a local covering.

So let me drop this into your spirit. Any situation or scenario that has come up against you to make you question the church or give up on the fellowship, is a trick of the enemy. The enemy works through people, so whoever did it was not operating in the Spirit of God. They were working on behalf of the enemy (some knowingly, some unknowingly.) The enemy is trying to block your from connecting with a local body because he knows that some of the your greatest lessons about life will come from your graduate study in the local church-a good Bible teaching church. So pray about where God has assigned, and go in understanding that we are all human, and if any situation or circumstance comes up to cause you to question the church, it is likely a trick of the enemy. Pray for the right fit. Pray for the right covering. Pray for a called, anointed, appointed and educated woman or man of God with common sense. Pray for your leadership to stretch you. Stretching increases your capacity and when you have an increase in capacity, you have room for more.

I come to you Wonderful Counselor
(Isaiah 9:6)

Father, in the name of Jesus, I come to lay my reservations before you. I love you. I believe you love me so much that you sent your son to die for me. But Lord I am conflicted in dealing with the church. I've experienced things internally/externally and now I am uncertain and tentative about what to do. Lord, I have this issue [name it _____] but I know your Word says we are not to give up meeting together and we are to submit to leaders and connect with a local body. I need You to resolve it, firm it in my spirit. Help me to get past the former things that have happened and help me to move boldly into honoring your command for a local covering. Help me to get beyond the people who are judgmental, unkind and unwelcoming so I can hear from you. Lord, help me to grow in my spiritual walk and release me from using my bad experience as an excuse to be lazy. I want to be planted somewhere with other strong believers. I want to be able to serve, give and grow into the woman you have created me to be. Do it, Lord. Show me my home and remove any residue that may taint or block my next level of access in you. I pray, in advance, for the Shepherd whom is contracted to cover me in this season of my life. In Jesus' Name. Amen.

The righteous man will flourish like the palm tree, He will grow like a cedar in Lebanon. Planted in the house of the LORD, They will flourish in the courts of our God. They will still yield fruit in old age; They shall be full of sap and very green. – Psalm 92:12-13

From whom the whole body, joined and held together by every joint with which it is equipped, when each part is working properly, makes the body grow so that it builds itself up in love. – Ephesians 4:16

Let all bitterness and wrath and anger and clamor and slander be put away from you, along with all malice. Be kind to one another, tenderhearted, forgiving one another, as God in Christ forgave you. – Ephesians 4:31-32

...Not giving up meeting together, as some are in the habit of doing, but encouraging one another--and all the more as you see the Day approaching. – Hebrews 10:25

Have confidence in your leaders and submit to their authority, because they keep watch over you as those who must give an account. Do this so that their work will be a joy, not a burden, for that would be of no benefit to you. – Hebrews 13:17

36
A prayer to resolve your worry

> *"Train up a child in the way he should go;*
> *even when he is old he will not depart from it."*
> **– Proverbs 22:6**

PARENTING MUST BE THE HARDEST JOB IN THE WORLD. YOU give birth, and you develop this overwhelming emotional attachment to this beautiful human being. But because of this attachment, the emotion that most persists through life for parents everywhere (no matter your race, status, or faith tradition) is fear for their children. I have seen my friends go through difficult seasons of heaviness (and even depression) out of concern for their children's wellbeing. I've seen worry and concern for children who have grown up in two-parent households. Even though they have the best of everything, they still wander down the dark road of distraction and lasciviousness. I've also seen worry and concern from single mothers who are trying to figure out every day how they will provide for their children. The biggest struggle I've seen, though, with parents is the transition period from one stage of parenting to another.

A few years ago, I had a conversation with a friend who was overwhelmed financially. He had two children in college, and the third child was about to enter into a very prestigious University.

But at the last minute, she decided to forgo that opportunity in order to travel across country. The parent was overwhelmed. I think he was also disappointed that his daughter did not follow the "normal" plan of a four-year university. He was covering the cost of her living expenses. So, in this scenario, I literally had to talk him off the ledge. He admitted that both he and his wife had done everything for their children. They also carried a lot of their student loan debt. But even worse than that, these parents were now questioning what was next for them.

This is one of the biggest misnomers in life. While there is no parent training university and no formal way to learn *how* to parent, I think so many parents do an amazing job in spite of not having the playbook. However, where parents fall short is in learning how to celebrate successful seasons and transitioning to the different levels of being a parent. In other words, for my friend who managed to get three children through high school and two through college, he had done a good job but he and his wife could not celebrate that. They couldn't honor the milestone because they were still stuck in the first stage of parenting.

If you managed to raise responsible children, then you have succeeded in the first task as a parent. The next step of parenting is to transition from primary care giver to guidance and direction. Once your children are grown, you transition to the second stage. You no longer make decisions for your children. You now have to trust that the work you did in the first season will be applied in the real world. When you are still attached to your adult children, you lean towards enabling rather than empowering them to grow into adulthood. You stifle their growth. It's okay to be available and on call for help and supervision, but you must step out of the leadership role and allow him/her to become the leader of his/her own life.

The lesson of releasing yourself from concern, worry and fear is necessary in order to save yourself. Worry can ruin your life. It can stress you out and wear you down. No matter what situation or circumstance your child may be in right now, whether there are issues of sickness and disease, unemployment, drugs, abuse, imprisonment, or mental illness, you have to manage that emotion before you can be of any use to your child(ren.) If you stay in a constant state of worry, you are demonstrating a lack of faith. The Word says do not be anxious about anything but in everything you should pray and be thankful and then let your request be made known to God.

God doesn't want you to worry about your children. Psalms 55 says give your burdens to the Lord and He will take care of you. He will not permit the Godly to slip and fall. After all, they are his children first and you are just the vessel. He allowed them to come through you however He is the provider of all things for all people. God is ultimately responsible for your children. He is the one who sees all and knows all and provides for all things. If you teach your children about Jesus when they are young, you will know that they have access to the same source that you have access to. And even if they don't know God, you can intercede for them. But not when you are worrying or misrepresenting God in your faith walk. You can control worry. Self-control is the fruit of the Spirit; for God gave us power, love and self-control (2 Timothy 1:7) If you are a believer (and I believe that you are), then you are called by God to walk in the fruit of the spirit, and to walk in integrity. The mere fact that God commanded you to do THIS says you have it within you to take control of your mind.

Worry is doubt and doubt cancels faith. Fear and faith cannot coexist. Fear about what could happen to your child cannot dwell in you if you are a believer. If you struggle with this, then know that you have your own growth and development to work through. Shift your time and attention from worry and concern about what your child is doing to time invested in building your faith so that God can teach you how to celebrate the stages of life in balance and abundance.

I come to you Prince of Peace
(Isaiah 9:6)

Father God in the name of Jesus, I come to you as a parent with a heavy/concerned heart. I confess that it is not easy to let go sometimes. It is not easy to switch gears. It is not easy to turn off the emotional strings of my heart when you are mother, but Lord, I ask you to remove the spirit of worry right now. My Faith is in you and I trust you. Help me to remember that no matter what, my child is your child. You gave him/her life and I trust you to keep him/her in the midst of it all. In Jesus' name. Amen

Casting all your anxieties on him, because he cares for you. – 1 Peter 5:7

Humble yourselves, therefore, under the mighty hand of God so that at the proper time he may exalt you, casting all your anxieties on him, because he cares for you. – 1 Peter 5:6-7

Anxiety in a man's heart weighs him down, but a good word makes him glad. – Proverbs 12:25

Peace I leave with you; my peace I give to you. Not as the world gives do I give to you. Let not your hearts be troubled, neither let them be afraid. – John 14:27

Anxiety in a man's heart weighs him down, but a good word makes him glad. – Proverbs 12:25

37

A prayer when you've been betrayed

> "For our struggle is not against flesh and blood,
> but against the rulers, against the authorities,
> against the powers of this dark world and against the
> spiritual forces of evil in the heavenly realms."
> – **Ephesians 6:12**

JESUS WAS BETRAYED. THAT'S ALL I COULD THINK ABOUT during a season in the beginning of my ministry were I had a "Judas" experience in the camp. You know the kind. You just extended your hand to invite someone in to your space and in the next moment, you have to extend that same arm long enough to grab the knife from your back. *Yes, that kind of betrayal.* A person very close to me was the enemy's choice representative to bring me to tears. But she taught me a valuable lesson that I needed to learn about leadership, ministry and jealously.

God gave me the assignment of a lifetime, and promoted me beyond my ability to ask or think and the interesting thing was, I was already working in the area of my gifting so I didn't see this promotion coming. But here I was praying for women all around the globe and with such favor in the first year, we went from 33 women to hundreds and then thousands. This movement was an unplanned initiative in response to hurting women struggling to get through a recession. In year one, we had massive growth, a large team, and an inaugural event that drew people from all over the country to New Jersey. We had a press conference on Capitol Hill, a radio platform and television exposure. We were invited to be part of a mission's journey and to partner with the White House Office on Faith Based Initiatives.

One of my team members was a minister in a small church. She was a prominent figure at the church (which had a membership of about 40) and now, she was at the top of a really attractive new ministry that was getting major play. The betrayal happened when she wanted to introduce an idea that did not line up with the ministry and I declined. It was not within the scope of the vision. And because this was a new ministry, I wanted to be responsible with what God had placed in my hands. Well, in that very short season and after a few weeks of trying to manage her out, people started to notice a spirit of jealously stirring up. They observed a noticeable shift in her attitude, demeanor and responses. But I turned my head for a minute knowing it was an attempt of the enemy to throw me off. I refused to look her way and sought wise counsel on how to manage that spirit. After she continued to take from the ministry to build her own ideas, I eventually asked her to leave. The funny thing is, it empowered her to start her own ministry and then she copied everything I did. In this situation, imitation was not the greatest form of flattery but the lowest form of *no originality*.

Having said that, let me drop this in your spirit: If you are setting out to do the will of God, expect betrayal. Expect to lose people. Expect to attract people who will come to you with the wrong motive. Expect people to steal from you and cause strife. Jesus was betrayed, so you too will be betrayed; and it's likely to happen by someone in the camp, otherwise it would not affect you. Not only should you expect betrayal, you must learn the lesson that it came to teach you. God can reveal purpose even in this. The betrayal was a power lesson for me. God allowed it in order to develop me, stretch me, grow me up and increase my capacity for more. Hallelujah for that lesson early in my ministry. The betrayal worked for my good and I don't hold the person responsible I know the enemy was and is at work to stop God's plan and purpose for my life. It's all good or God will use it for good.

I come to you omnipresent God
(Proverbs 15:3)

Father, in the name of Jesus, I lay this betrayal before you and I seek you for resolve. Lord, see my heart and know that I am hurt, crushed and disappointed. My heart is damaged and I come to you to fix it. My mind is doing backflips about why and how {insert name} could do this to me. Help me, Lord to sit still and to receive whatever lesson you have in this situation. Lord, I know you are with me and I know your ways are not like my ways. I know you are working all things out for my good. Lord I know your Word says to release the stronghold so I can forgive them, pray for them and move on. Help me to be mature enough to know your Word and heed the warning that my struggle is not against flesh and blood but against the rulers, against the authorities, against the powers of this dark world and against the spiritual forces of evil in the heavenly realms, Help me expect it, pray in advance about it and to handle it decently and in order. In Jesus' Name, Amen

For our struggle is not against flesh and blood, but against the rulers, against the authorities, against the powers of this dark world and against the spiritual forces of evil in the heavenly realms. – Ephesians 6:12

The Lord said to my Lord: "Sit at my right hand until I put your enemies under your feet. – Matthew 22:44

For if you forgive other people when they sin against you, your heavenly Father will also forgive you. – Matthew 6:14

Beloved, never avenge yourselves, but leave it to the wrath of God, for it is written, "Vengeance is mine, I will repay, says the Lord." To the contrary, "if your enemy is hungry, feed him; if he is thirsty, give him something to drink; for by so doing you will heap burning coals on his head." Do not be overcome by evil, but overcome evil with good. – Romans 12:19-21

"But I say to you who hear, Love your enemies, do good to those who hate you, bless those who curse you, pray for those who abuse you. To one who strikes you on the cheek, offer the other also, and from one who takes away your cloak do not withhold your tunic either. Give to everyone who begs from you, and from one who takes away your goods do not demand them back. And as you wish that others would do to you, do so to them. – Luke 6:27-36

38

A prayer to overcome fear

So I RAN INTO THREE WOMEN ONE DAY AT THE TOP OF AN escalator trying to map out a path so they wouldn't have to get on the escalator. Turns out, one of the three women developed a fear of heights after a fall of some sort. But the interesting thing is, they were all wearing badges for a local church conference, which was an indication that they were believers. *(*Pregnant Pause)* I'll get to the reason for my pause in just a minute. But that was my cue or shall I say the nudge in my spirit to say something… So of course, I asked for permission to chat with the ladies and to share my own fears with them (*I have a fear of cats, public speaking and being sprayed by a skunk. Don't judge me.*) Yes. I used to be afraid of lots of things but not any more. I learned how to overcome my fear and was able to see the Word of God become a reality in my heart.

Here's the interesting thing about my encounter with those women. My first reaction, after hearing their stories, was empathy. I felt bad for these ladies and I thought about the manifold opportunities they've missed as a result of fear. My second observation was that they were all believers of Christ, attending a church conference about Jesus but challenged in trusting God and honoring the Word of God. The third issue was when I asked the woman "are you believing God for some things or believing Him to move in your life?" Of course, she responded "yes." So I said, "How is it that you can believe Him for some things but not all things?" I told her whatever she's believing God for is just outside of her comfort zone. Living with fear is like living in bondage. You become a slave to the thing that takes your courage. When you live in bondage, you don't have the freedom to be, to do, or to go as you please. Over time, there must be progress. You must move from fear to courage over time, and the only way to do that is to pray about it. I do believe in miracles, but I also believe in doing the necessary work so that we can conquer our fears.

Greatness let me drop this in your spirit. If you are struggling with fear right now, you have to know you are not alone. It is normal for human beings to have and feel fear. Fear is an emotion that serves a significant purpose. When used appropriately, it can warn you and help you to discern danger. Fear is also an emotion controlled by our thinking. You feel free when you give attention to the thing that frightens you. Some people get over fear, stand in fear or walk boldly through it. But the bottom line is, we all experience it. It is critical for you as a believer to come to a place of having no fear except in God Himself. That is a non-negotiable for every believer in Christ, otherwise we fall into the stereotypical believer who says she loves the Lord but doesn't do what the Lord says. You have to overcome it and how you do that will take faith and work.

I come to you Prince of Peace
(Isaiah 9:6)

Father, in the name of Jesus, I come to you right now realizing I need help. Lord, I admit I am living with fear and faith. I now know it is impossible to for the two to reside in the same space so I choose faith. I call out fear right now and say fear be gone in the name of Jesus. God did not allow fear so I accept the resolve in my walk to release it right now. Lord help be to let go of childhood fears. Help me to keep watch over the gate of my mind to see clearly the thoughts that don't line up with your Word in Philippians 4:8. I believe you sent your son to die for me. I believe in Jesus the Christ. I believe I will go to heaven one day, but while I was proclaiming to believe in you, I was also blinded by the fact that I have been out of order. I have allowed fear to get in the way of my faith. Help me, Lord. In Jesus' name. Amen.

For God gave us a spirit not of fear but of power and love and self-control. – 2 Timothy 1:7

Fear not, for I am with you; be not dismayed, for I am your God; I will strengthen you, I will help you, I will uphold you with my righteous right hand. – Isaiah 41:10

I sought the Lord, and he answered me and delivered me from all my fears. – Psalm 34:4

Have I not commanded you? Be strong and courageous. Do not be frightened, and do not be dismayed, for the Lord your God is with you wherever you go." – Joshua 1:9

Be watchful, stand firm in the faith, act like men, be strong. – 1 Corinthians 16:13

39

A prayer against mental illness

*"So his fame spread throughout all Syria,
and they brought him all the sick, those afflicted with
various diseases and pains, those oppressed by demons,
epileptics, and paralytics, and he healed them."*
- Matthew 4:24

WHAT DO YOU DO WHEN SOMETHING WEIRD IS HAPPENING in your head but you have no frame of reference for it? What do you do when signs of mental imbalance show themselves and you don't know what to call it? If you've ever encountered someone who was called "crazy" or if you've struggled with mental illness, then, my sister, we need to pray on this matter.

The reference "crazy" is a childhood impression I held on to until I was an adult. I learned that "crazy" was associated with weird people who did odd things and unique behavior that was not typical of most. It wasn't until I enrolled in a graduate course in Abnormal Psychology that I was able to better understand the misunderstood. It was one lesson in that class that forever changed my perception of what most people call "crazy." I learned the difference between normal people and abnormal people who suffer from mental illness. The major difference between the two is intensity and duration of a pre-existing state of being. The example the professor gave revealed a very thin line between the person who suffers from an imbalance and those who don't. It enlightened me. It saddened me. It softened my heart towards those who suffer. It humbled me knowing that God had protected my mind because it could have been me.

So here's what I know about the struggle with mental illness. Whether you or your loved one is dealing with some sort of psychological defect like depression, bi-polar, anxiety disorder, attention deficit/hyperactivity disorder or dissociate disorders like amnesia, fugue or identity disorder, feeding & eating disorders, sexual, paraphilia disorders to stuttering, whatever your challenge is right now, know that mental abnormality is real. You don't need to OWN what may be happening in your head. But you don't want to deny what may be happening in your head. Don't be ashamed or embarrassed. You are not "crazy." There may be a chemical imbalance in your system, but yet and still you are a child of the Most High. There may be a break in your internal wiring and that's not an imaginary thing. Yet and still you are God's creation and He made you fearfully and wonderfully made. You may have been told "it's all in your head" or "that's just the enemy" or "shake it off" but be mindful that whoever has spoken that into your spirit is just ill-informed, uneducated and scared by negative childhood impressions of mental illness. You are who God says you are. You don't need to OWN it but you must acknowledge what you are experiencing so you can address it. Address the issue in the spiritual and in the natural. So many people die out of ignorance. You can live if you deal with this and ask God to deliver you and make your way to get help. Don't live in denial allowing the issue to go unaddressed. Don't deny what's happening. Don't be embarrassed or ashamed. Don't listen to people who are not equipped, trained, licensed or qualified to speak on these matter. Run don't walk to the nearest mental health professional who is trained and licensed. Continue to pray and trust God. He will bring peace to your mind, in Jesus' name.

I come to you Great Physician
(Luke 4:23)

Father, in the name of Jesus, Your Word says in Psalm 34:17-20 "When the righteous cry for help, the Lord hears and delivers them out of all their troubles. The Lord is near to the broken-hearted and saves the crushed in spirit. Many are the afflictions of the righteous, but the Lord delivers him out of them all. He keeps all his bones; not one of them is broken." Now God please hear my cry and deliver me from whatever chemical imbalance or mental disorder and abnormality that may be present. Open my eyes, my ears and my spirit that I may be aware of what's happening with me rather than consumed by what's happening around me. I know you to be a healer. So I call on You, Jehovah Rapha. You are the God of the impossible and nothing is outside of your reach. Give me direction on next steps and resources (whether it includes physicians, counseling or therapy.) Give me resolve about the diagnoses if you approve, Lord. I trust that you are the great physician and I choose to believe your report. Help me not to be ignorant or to fall into stereotypical cultural patterns of denial. I need you to resolve in my heart what the diagnosis may be and the appropriate treatment, if necessary. And if Lord, this is nothing but a battle of spiritual forces fighting to win me to the enemy's team, I speak forth faith right now. I declare that Jesus is My Lord and Savior and the entire substitutionary work done at the cross was for me. The enemy and his assignment is null, void, canceled, yanked and destroyed at the root right now in Jesus' Name. My mind is stable; my thinking is sound, the inner workings of my biological make up are operating at 100% and cooperating with the plan and purposes of God, in Jesus' Name.

When the righteous cry for help, the Lord hears and delivers them out of all their troubles. The Lord is near to the brokenhearted and saves the crushed in spirit. Many are the afflictions of the righteous, but the Lord delivers him out of them all. He keeps all his bones; not one of them is broken. – Psalm 34:17-20

Do not be anxious about anything, but in everything by prayer and supplication with thanksgiving let your requests be made known to God. And the peace of God, which surpasses all understanding, will guard your hearts and your minds in Christ Jesus. – Philippians 4:6-7

So his fame spread throughout all Syria, and they brought him all the sick, those afflicted with various diseases and pains, those oppressed by demons, epileptics, and paralytics, and he healed them. – Matthew 4:24

For God gave us a spirit not of fear but of power and love and self-control. – 2 Timothy 1:7

I have said these things to you, that in me you may have peace. In the world you will have tribulation. But take heart; I have overcome the world." – John 16:33

40

A prayer when you are disconnected from church

> *"Judge not, and you will not be judged;*
> *condemn not, and you will not be condemned;*
> *forgive, and you will be forgiven;*
> *– Luke 6:37*

I'M SITTING IN CHURCH READY TO RECEIVE. I'M WAITING on the pastor and waiting on the Word. I'm waiting for God to speak and waiting for the spirit to move and… nothing. Absolutely nothing. I'm actually visiting a church; one that I had visited before but on this particular day, there's a lot of talk and the minister did not deliver a scripture and the sermon sounds more like a very practical motivational speech. Now that would be fine on most days and in other settings, but today is the Lord's Day. And I'm hungry for the Lord. In fact, I think there were some other folks hungry for something different than what was on the menu and they walked out.

Have you ever felt that way? Have you ever pressed your way to church excited and anxious about what God was going to say to you when you got there? And when you got there, the church was serving something different? Well I know that it has happened to me on a few occasions. In my younger years, I was a little more judgmental. When you are a baby in Christ, you tend to be that way. But when you grow in your spiritual walk, your appetite matures in such a way that you become open to receiving God however God chooses to show up to speak. So on the day I found myself again starving, I began to exercise my faith and apply my lessons learned.

I have learned in situations where you are with a body of believers and the Word is not delivered in a manner to which you are accustomed that it is your responsibility to work through that. It is not an issue of the church or the pastor. Remember, God has not given us permission to judge even in the church, *especially* in the church. It is not for you to say what it is not. It isn't your job to discuss whether he or she is qualified, called or ordained. It is a better position to take your issue to the Lord even while you're sitting in the pew. Voice your grievance to the Lord and ask God to shift your heart so you can receive whatever God wants you to receive through that vessel. Realize it may not be what you think. It may be God presenting an opportunity to stretch you even when it appears that you are spiritually malnourished. Bottom line we are to pray and receive the lesson.

I come to you Lord of All
(Acts 10:36)

Father God in the name of Jesus, I lay before you my spiritual appetite, my desire for more substance and my need to receive the Word in a particular way. Lord, forgive me for judging/critiquing/complaining about the church. Grow me out of that shallow walk and diversify my appetite. Remove any stereotypical desires for church in a certain way so I can sit with an open heart and receive from whatever instrument you choose to use to speak to me. I want to be the woman you created me to be. I want to live according to your plan in Jeremiah 29:11. I want to see growth in my walk that I may be a better witness for you. Thank you for allowing me to put all of my expectations in you. Make me a mature Christian in Jesus' name, Amen.

"Judge not, and you will not be judged; condemn not, and you will not be condemned; forgive, and you will be forgiven; – Luke 6:37

Do not judge by appearances, but judge with right judgment." – John 7:24

Do not speak evil against one another, brothers. The one who speaks against a brother or judges his brother, speaks evil against the law and judges the law. But if you judge the law, you are not a doer of the law but a judge. There is only one lawgiver and judge, he who is able to save and to destroy. But who are you to judge your neighbor? – James 4:11-12

The aim of our charge is love that issues from a pure heart and a good conscience and a sincere faith. – 1 Timothy 1:5

For God alone, O my soul, wait in silence, for my hope is from him. – Psalm 62:5

41

A prayer to be
used by God

> "Jabez cried out to the God of Israel, "Oh that you would
> bless me and enlarge my territory! Let your hand be with
> me, and keep me from harm so that I will be free from
> pain." And God granted his request."
> **– 1 Chronicles 4:10**

S O MANY WOMEN HAVE A BURNING DESIRE TO LEAD. I SEE
women who desire promotion and high levels of leadership
in their respective jobs. I see women who desire to run their own
enterprises. I see women who have been called to ministry. The one
common thread, no matter where you are in terms of your vocation,
is that all of us want to do well. In fact, you don't want to survive
in the area of your work, you want to thrive! We are now living
in a time where more woman have become bold and unapologetic
about wanting to be the best, have the most, ascend to the highest
level, and live on top of the world. And that's how it should be. You
will never achieve beyond the level of your thinking. If you think
big, then your chances of being a high achiever, a game changer, a
power-player and the best ambassador for Christ are greater.

If you're like most, you are probably trying to figure out how
to accomplish your goals. You are seeking success in business,

success as an entrepreneur or success in ministry. One of the things that I have learned about becoming successful, no matter what it is that you do, is to pray first. I've been asked on occasion, "How did you achieve such success as an entrepreneur and as a ministry leader with a global ministry of over 100,000 women around the world?" My response is prayer. I don't mean that I prayed and asked God to promote me on my job, or to make me a business owner over the masses. I had a different conversation with God. *I asked God to use me.* I volunteered myself and God blessed me in that posture of service. When you pray that kind of prayer of surrender, God will promote you on your job. God will make room for your gift. God will elevate you to positions of leadership. God will qualify you where you don't meet the requirements. God will enlarge your territory. I am a witness: after praying my own prayer of Jabez "God, show me how to take who I am, who I want to be and what I can do and use it for a purpose greater than myself." I encourage you to pray for service and not for success (that God would give you an assignment), and God will hear your prayer and do it for you.

I come to you God of the Whole Earth
(Isaiah 54:5)

Father, in the name of Jesus, I come before you Lord God to thank you for the privilege and the opportunity to tap into your power. Lord I'm grateful to be called daughter of the most high and to have access to you Lord. Thank you for the desires that you have planted in my heart to succeed. Thank you Lord for stirring up something in my spirit that calls me higher. Thank you Lord for the possibility to win in whatever I lay my hands to. Now God bless the work of my hands. Give me favor in whatever work you call me to do. Make a way of entry or a way of opportunity for me in places where the world says there is a glass ceiling. Lord I surrender my hands, my heart, my head, my feet, my mouth, and my very being to your will. Use me Lord for greater. Show me how to take who I am, who I want to be, and what I can do and use it for a purpose greater than myself. In Jesus' name, Amen.

The LORD will open the heavens, the storehouse of his bounty, to send rain on your land in season and to bless all the work of your hands. You will lend to many nations but will borrow from none. – Deuteronomy 28:12.

The LORD your God has blessed you in all the work of your hands. He has watched over your journey through this vast wilderness. These forty years the LORD your God has been with you, and you have not lacked anything. – Deuteronomy 2:7

Jabez cried out to the God of Israel, "Oh that you would bless me and enlarge my territory! Let your hand be with me, and keep me from harm so that I will be free from pain." And God granted his request. – 1 Chronicles 4:10

Whatever you do, work heartily, as for the Lord and not for men, knowing that from the Lord you will receive the inheritance as your reward. You are serving the Lord Christ. – Colossians 3:23-24

But remember the LORD your God, for it is he who gives you the ability to produce wealth, and so confirms his covenant, which he swore to your ancestors, as it is today. – Deuteronomy 8:18

42

A prayer when your feelings are hurt by rejection

*"Whoever does not receive you, nor heed your words,
as you go out of that house or that city,
shake the dust off your feet."*
– Matthew 10:14

I F YOU ARE THE KIND OF PERSON THAT IS EASILY OFFENDED and hurt by someone else's actions, I want to share my own personal lesson with you. Hopefully, it will help you to break free from the chains of sensitivity and rejection. If someone has said or done something hurtful to you, know this: you get to decide how you will respond. You get to decide what you will do with that information because the truth of the matter is. It is information and not fact. What people say about you is not sacred gospel, it is their human opinion. Whatever you receive from others is subjective based on his/her own filters. You have no idea what goes on behind the scenes, so do not take everything at face value.

I used to be a person with thin skin. I used to take everything personal. However, I remember the shift of learning a powerful lesson about other people's actions. And that lesson was simple: it's not about you. If someone says something about you, it's not necessarily a jab at you or an attack against you. Their response could be based on how they see the world, their view, their filters, their values, goals and challenges. Think about it. Have you ever responded to something and it was perceived as an offense, but the truth is, there was something going on with you.

My mother shared a story with me once that I will never forget. She decided not to attend her best friend's husband's birthday party and her girlfriend was offended by her absence. Well my mother said she was on a health regimen and in order to remain disciplined, she couldn't be in a social environment. So her "no" had nothing to do with her girlfriend or the husband. It had nothing to do with her not liking them. It was more about her and less about them. You see, many people respond to things based on what's going on with them. Now there are times when an offense is about you? Yes, I'm sure it happens, but not always.

I remember asking someone to do something and their response was no. Well immediately, my feelings were hurt. I didn't even process the response or think about it. I was just hurt considering this was someone who had said yes before, so I was taken aback when they wouldn't agree. Moments later, I found myself going back to "Dee it's not about you. Why are you taking it personal? You have no idea what's behind her response." See, we have a tendency to make things up in our heads that aren't necessarily true. Like, if someone has offended you and there's no real knowing behind the offense, you start making things up. You conjure up negative or bad thoughts, but the problem with that line of thinking is that none of it is true. You've made it up, and that doesn't line up with God's Word "whatever things are true whatever things are noble whatever things are righteous whatever things are admirable whatever things or praiseworthy think on such things." We tend to make up bad stuff.

What should you do when you're offended? Remember, life is 10% what happens to you and 90% how you respond to it. You get to choose how you respond to others. It's not always about you. Don't take everything personal. Give yourself time to think and to pray. Resist the temptation to overanalyzing. Ask God to guard your heart, firm your skin and resolve any insecurity within you. My sister surrender your feelings to God in prayer and be truthful.

I come to you God my Rock
(1 Corinthians 10:4)

Father, in the name of Jesus, I come before you God because I am offended. I'm sorry that I feel this way but I do. My feelings were hurt and I'm tired of feeling this way. I don't want to be affected or moved by the actions of other people. Lord, help me to resolve my insecurity. Lord, help me to not take everything so personal. Enable me to walk in the fruit of the Spirit that gives me the power of self control. Help me to live according to your standard and to think on positive things. I now see that it is a scheme of the enemy to keep me hurt but I resist it right now in Jesus' name. I have the mind of Christ. I have the power of self-control and the ability to choose my thoughts and guide my emotions. Change me, Lord. Transform me into the woman you have created me to be so that I am never offended, but I am able to move forward in confidence. In Jesus' name Amen

A brother offended is more unyielding than a strong city, and quarreling is like the bars of a castle. – Proverbs 18:19

Know this, my beloved brothers: let every person be quick to hear, slow to speak, slow to anger; – James 1:19

See to it that no one fails to obtain the grace of God; that no "root of bitterness" springs up and causes trouble, and by it many become defiled; – Hebrews 12:15

"Whoever does not receive you, nor heed your words, as you go out of that house or that city, shake the dust off your feet. – Matthew 10:14

The heart is deceitful above all things, and desperately sick; who can understand it? – Jeremiah 17:9

43

A prayer when you've been publicly humiliated

> "More than that, we rejoice in our sufferings,
> knowing that suffering produces endurance,
> and endurance produces character, and character
> produces hope, and hope does not put us to shame,
> because God's love has been poured into our hearts
> through the Holy Spirit who has been given to us."
> **– Romans 5:3-5**

DRUGS, JAIL, ADDICTION, EVICTION, REJECTION, DIVORCE, adultery, sickness or disease and bankruptcy... Have you ever had a scandal in your life that caused pain, shame, embarrassment or humiliation? Well, recently my senses became more aware when we received this heart-wrenching letter at the ministry. A woman wrote in about a domino of humiliation that started when her father who jumped out of the window was found outside naked from a drug overdose induced heart attack. Then, to make matters worse, people uploaded the picture to Facebook. Publicly humiliated, the downward spiral resulted in her gaining over 40 pounds, it reawakened her own addiction to drugs, and she ended up evicted from her home and living in a shelter with two children. Again, some heartless people took pictures of her and posted them on Facebook. I have heard many stories in the ministry, but never had I heard of this level of shame attached to someone else's downfall.

Now your situation may not be as appalling as this one, but you may resonate with the feelings associated with shame, if that is the case, then consider how you can survive any dishonor that may visit your home. The first place to run is prayer. After that, there are practical life strategies you must consider in order to stay sane and not succumb to the temptation of beating yourself up.

To get through your most horrendous, unexpected, unwanted, dreadful realities, you have to manage your emotions in real time. In some instances, you may have a confidante. In other instances, you will need to sit silently by yourself and process your emotions without background noise. Background noise from those around you can overshadow your thoughts and block the voice of the Lord. Have you ever noticed how distracting it is when people make your pain about them? That's what I'm talking about. Silence the incoming traffic. Put your big girl panties on and get in your private prayer closet. Deal with your emotions before you invite other people in. Guard and protect your inner most thoughts and feelings from people who have not earned the right to your story. You have to be able to stand on top of the story when you tell it. Acknowledge how you are feeling. If you are feeling shame or embarrassment or hurt or discomfort, journal that. You don't need to own it, but you do need to acknowledge it. You cannot fix what you do not acknowledge.

Your fix is going to come over time as you breathe, walk, pray and process. When you get the phone call that feels like a gut punch, the first thing you must do is breathe in and out. Sounds ridiculous, but you need to concentrate your focus. Intentional breaths will help you to gather yourself. Next, you should walk gently. It will reduce the chances of reacting in haste. Getting control over your emotions will put you in a better posture to be led by God. When you are not in control of your emotions, noise and clutter will try to cloud your judgment. When a cloud is hovering over you, the enemy will try to steal everything you thought you were progressing toward. Pray en route to therapy. Process your feelings with a licensed therapist. This is how you can come out of your shame and embarrassment. Pray without ceasing.

I come to you Master
(Luke 5:5)

Father, in the name of Jesus, I come before you right now in a low state. I ask that you lift my head. I am feeling such shame and embarrassment. I have no words to describe my hurt but you have given me words and a reason to hope. Would you help me resolve my issues and give me the direction on how to handle, respond and deal with people. Would you please speak on my behalf; script my language to be graceful when I have to answer to people. Would you cause the people who are witness to be kind, compassionate and understanding in this time? I need you Lord to lead me now. Lord, I know this is not the end of my story. I declare and decree your greatest work is in front of me. I declare and I decree that my latter shall be greater than my former. You never do your best work in the past, God. I know you to do exceedingly and abundantly above all I could think or ask. I believe no ear has heard nor eye has seen what you have in store for me. So I am believing by faith which is the substance of what I hope for with no evidence in sight. There is no evidence of a brighter day right now but I believe by faith that you can hear my cry and will come to my rescue. I believe you are at work in my life. Hide me from the enemy. I know you have a plan for my life. I believe you will restore me in Jesus' name, Amen.

Beloved, do not be surprised at the fiery trial when it comes upon you to test you, as though something strange were happening to you. But rejoice insofar as you share Christ's sufferings, that you may also rejoice and be glad when his glory is revealed. – 1 Peter 4:12-13

For "everyone who calls on the name of the Lord will be saved." – Romans 10:13

And after you have suffered a little while, the God of all grace, who has called you to his eternal glory in Christ, will himself restore, confirm, strengthen, and establish you. – 1 Peter 5:10

Count it all joy, my brothers, when you meet trials of various kinds, for you know that the testing of your faith produces steadfastness. And let steadfastness have its full effect, that you may be perfect and complete, lacking in nothing. – James 1:2-4

For I consider that the sufferings of this present time are not worth comparing with the glory that is to be revealed to us. – Romans 8:18

44

A prayer for the holiday and dysfunctional family gatherings

> *"Bear with each other and forgive one another if any of you has a grievance against someone. Forgive as the Lord forgave you."*
> **– Colossians 3:13**

I WISH I HAD MAYBE JUST ONE CRAZY THANKSGIVING DINNER table story of an off-the-wall uncle or out of order cousin, but that isn't my experience. To be honest, now that I really think about it, crazy family stories are only entertaining if they happen at someone else's house. The sad situation is, there are many holiday gatherings where crazy things happen between family members that ruin people forever.

I'll never forget the prayer request we received as a precursor to Thanksgiving. I remember women sharing unbelievable scenarios like having to be in the same room with the family member who secretly molested her as a young child, or I've heard stories of women and their exes and the thought of having to come face-to-face with the other woman because of the holiday drop off and pick up arrangement. And then of course there are many other unbearable situations like the matriarch or patriarch who is missing from the table because they have transitioned. Whatever your discomfort or family dysfunction is, the good news is, you can deal with it better if you pray.

One of the strategies you may need to use in preparation for holiday gatherings is this: deal with it head on before the gathering. Think about what the event is typically like and then pinpoint the triggers that lead to your discomfort. Once you have clarity on how the situation may unfold, you can map out your response. Life is 10% what happens and 90% how we respond. You can choose to do something different than what you've done in the past. You can choose to engage in the negative chitchat, or you can choose to remain silent. You can choose to speak only words that are positive and encouraging, or you can choose to add fuel to the fire. You can choose to let God use you or you can give into the temptation of the enemy who obviously wants to steal, kill and destroy the spirit of your family. We are human creatures of choice and you have the ability to make a different choice.

I recommend you give careful thought to this prior to any family gathering. You become a better person when you carefully think and consider your actions in advance. Typically, when most people show up in a fit of rage or anger, he or she is reacting in real time based on emotions. Move away from reacting and doing or saying something that you may regret, and shift to thinking about your standard beforehand. Then, choose to respond differently. If you really want to step up your game, remember the greatness that God has called you to be. Debrief yourself at the end of the night. Ask yourself, "am I proud of how I showed up today? Was I part of the problem or was I part of the solution? Did I respond or did I react?" Was I decent and in order according to God's word in 1 Corinthians 14:40? Did I honor God's command to love my neighbors?

I come to you Merciful God
(Jeremiah 3:12)

Father, in the name of Jesus, I come before you to ask for a sweet resolve during this holiday gathering. Lord, the issue is [name the issue] among [name the individuals involved] and it's no longer acceptable. Father, in my desire for more of you and growth along the spiritual journey, I am now sensitive to familial situations that are unhealthy, risky, painful and disheartening. You see my coming and my going. You know when I lie down and when I wake up. For that reason, Lord I trust that you see all sides of the equation. Nothing is hidden from you. So, now God, in your divine wisdom and insight would you please move in me and through me this holiday? Transform me and allow me to be your representative at the gathering. Prepare me now in advance to set a standard that matches up with your standard in Philippians 4:9. Lord, help me to think like you think and to speak like you speak. I don't want to be churchy or a super Christian but I do want to be the best Ambassador for you. Lord help me to walk in the fruit of the Spirit. Your word says it and I believe that I have self-control, patience, and kindness in me. Let your peace rest in me. Go ahead of me. Meet me at the dinner table. Thank you for lifting the cloud of grief and mourning from the gathering. Lord I intercede on behalf of every family member. I pray for deliverance. I pray for salvation. I pray for a break of generational curses. I pray for a release from addiction, adultery and negative talk. I pray in advance for the finances needed to cover the cost of feeding everyone and even extra to give to the needy. Lord I thank you for stretching me and for better days to come with family. In Jesus' Name Amen

Bear with each other and forgive one another if any of you has a grievance against someone. Forgive as the Lord forgave you. – Colossians 3:13

And he answered, "You shall love the Lord your God with all your heart and with all your soul and with all your strength and with all your mind, and your neighbor as yourself." – Luke 10:27

If you love me, you will keep my commandments. – John 14:15

Whoever claims to love God yet hates a brother or sister is a liar. For whoever does not love their brother and sister, whom they have seen, cannot love God, whom they have not seen. – 1 John 4:20

Like a muddied spring or a polluted fountain is a righteous man who gives way before the wicked. – Proverbs 25:26

45

A prayer when you need God to do it for you

> "But he said to me, "My grace is sufficient for you,
> for my power is made perfect in weakness."
> Therefore I will boast all the more gladly about my
> weaknesses, so that Christ's power may rest on me."
> **– 2 Corinthians 12:19**

I REMEMBER READING A BOOK ABOUT PRAYER AND FOR THE first time learning the power of divine enablement. Have you ever had major revelation about your own disobedience against God's will but you really wanted to be in God's will? In other words, have you ever struggled with something like forgiveness or tithing or serving or being more diligent in prayer? And have you ever said to yourself, "I want to forgive, I want to get the idea of tithing, or I want to serve, or I want to pray more, but I'm just not there right now?" It's like you want to be a fabulous, thin, curvy or healthy girl and you have an idea of what you're going to have to give up and what you're going to have to do in order to get there, but you're not ready to go there just yet. Another example (although it may be a stretch) but when you have a bad habit, you want to shake it. So you may smoke but in your heart, you are saying, "God I want to quit. Can you do it for me? If it's going to happen, you are going to have the do it." That requires the power of prayer for God to enable you to quit smoking. It's when you just don't feel capable and you need God to move on your behalf; it's when your heart is willing but your flesh week... that is when you have an awesome opportunity to throw your hands up in total dependence on God.

All of this simply means you need help and you can't do it on your own. But the good news is, you have your Father in Heaven who is able to do anything but fail. While it is true that God gives us the fruit of the Spirit, the manifestation of love, joy, peace, kindness, goodness, gentleness and self-control...all of this does not happen overnight. In other words, even though we are human creatures of choice and the word of God says that we as believers have the ability to think for ourselves, it is not without work that we begin to walk in the fruit of the spirit. So understand it takes work. And when your flesh is weak, ask God to enable you. Ask God to facilitate the breakthrough process of whatever you were struggling with. He will deliver you. He will help you. It is written God is faithful.

I come to you El-Roi
(Genesis 16:13)

Father God in the name of Jesus, I come before you to lay down my struggle with [fill in the blank]. Lord, you see my heart and you know my heart. I confess that I am not perfect, but I desire to live according to your word in Philippians 4:9 which says to follow your lead and do what you do. I know my issue is not from you and that you have called me higher. I know any personal slight or disobedience does not glorify you and it blocks my access to you. My desire is to be better and to do better in life. My desire is to take off my old self, my old habits, my old issues and anything that does not line up with what you have for me. So would you transform me and empower me now to loose the stronghold of [fill on the blank]. I know nothing is too hard for you. All things are possible because I believe. So now, God, line up my heart with my mind, thoughts, will and my behavior. Enable me now. I thank you for victory in advance. In Jesus' name, I pray amen.

But the fruit of the spirit is love, joy, peace, patience, kindness, goodness, faithfulness, gentleness, self-control; against such things there is no law... – Galatians 5:22-23

But he said to me, "My grace is sufficient for you, for my power is made perfect in weakness." Therefore I will boast all the more gladly about my weaknesses, so that Christ's power may rest on me. – 2 Corinthians 12:19

Watch and pray so that you will not fall into temptation. The spirit is willing, but the flesh is weak. – Matthew 26:19

When the righteous cry for help, the Lord hears and delivers them out of all their troubles. – Psalm 34:17

Consequently, he is able to save to the uttermost those who draw near to God through him, since he always lives to make intercession for them. – Hebrews 7:25

46

A prayer when you need peace and control

> "How can a young man keep his way pure?
> By guarding it according to your word."
> – Psalm 119:9

"SORRY, I'LL HAVE TO CALL YOU BACK." THESE WORDS can change your life. They may seem insignificant, however these words in many situations represent balance and control over your own life. I was standing at my bathroom sink putting on make-up before work and I got a call. The call came in from one of my favorite girls whom I love love love and adore. *Did I say love?* Yes one of my favorite people. Typically I don't answer the telephone before 9 AM, however I picked up the phone. My intention in picking up the phone was to make sure everything was okay because a call at this hour could be important. So we exchanged pleasantries and I found out that there was nothing pressing (which is good) and then after exchanging small talk, my favorite favorite favorite person goes into second gear to another random topic.... *Whoa whoa whoa pump the brakes.* "Hey I'm on my way out to work so I can't talk right now." Could I have continued on with the conversation in the process of handling my own business at home? Probably, but it wasn't anything critical. The conversation would've taken me out of focus. The chitchat would've been the switch to shut off my personal quiet time. That switch means "ok, world come on in" and I wasn't ready for that. I didn't want to be forced to open myself up to the world at that moment.

My point is this... In order to have peace in your life, you must be intentional about managing your life and controlling your day (the things that you can control.) You can no longer be a passenger allowing the events of the day to drive and set your course; you have to be the driver of your life. A lot of people have no peace in life and are unhappy because of this subtle but significant way of existing.

Having peace and gaining control over chaos, confusion and disorder requires that you take responsibility for your life goals and for everything that happens within 24 hours of this day. God blesses life in time increments of 86,400 seconds every day. It's his time not your time to waste; it is your time to manage, and you must do it decently and in order. If your life is out if control, it may be because your days are out of order. It's your responsibility to fix. The word of God says, "I have given you authority to rule." When you feel a lack of peace, a lack of control, out of balance, stretched and stressed could it be that you have not taken authority over your world? You have dominion over your world. You have permission to rule and regulate your life and everything that comes into your personal space. You have the power to call everything into order that was once out of order. You have the ability to set the agenda that best lines up with what you want to happen and to craft your own policy to support your best life.

When I disconnected from that call that was me exercising my right to create order. Some may judge this way of being, but I tell you the truth: this is how you stay sane. Allow God to stretch you in this chapter and take authority over your peace.

I come to you Armor of the Lord
(Isaiah 53:11)

Father, in the name of Jesus, I come before you to give honor to your name. God, I lay before you my life in days. I present to you my 24 hour day and how I move. Lord, I want peace in my life. Lord, I want to move about my day in a way that would glorify you. Enable me to silence the incoming traffic. Guard and protect my mind and my thoughts. Lord God, I have so much coming in to my personal space and so much that is placed on me that I need your help to manage. Lord God, let me see myself as you see me so I can learn how to boldly take a stand. Allow me to plan my day rather than allowing the circumstances of the world to control my life. Let me be gentle but effective when I have to stand up to family and friends who are loving, but draining. Would you intervene and guide my lips in difficult conversations? Grant me peace. Order my day. Take over my agenda. Move out of the way anything that is not life giving or serving. Help me to be better guided by your precepts. In Jesus' Name. Amen.

If possible, so far as it depends on you, live peaceably with all. – Romans 12:18

And he said to them, "Come away by yourselves to a desolate place and rest a while." For many were coming and going, and they had no leisure even to eat. – Mark 6:31

Therefore, if anyone is in Christ, he is a new creation. The old has passed away; behold, the new has come. – 2 Corinthians 5:17

For God is not a God of disorder but of peace--as in all the congregations of the Lord's people. – 1 Corinthians 14:33

Nevertheless, each person should live as a believer in whatever situation the Lord has assigned to them, just as God has called them. This is the rule I lay down in all the churches. – 1 Corinthians 7:17

47
A prayer when you are primary caregiver

> *"Humble yourselves, therefore, under the mighty hand of God so that at the proper time he may exalt you, casting all your anxieties on him, because he cares for you."*
> **– 1 Peter 5:6-7**

I WAS LITERALLY ON MY WAY TO A SHINDIG AT ESSENCE FEST when I remembered that I owed a call to one of my girls. Earlier that day, I got a "can you talk" text from her, and one thing about me, I may take forever to return a call, but when my people send for me on personal matters of the heart or a cry for help, I respond. On this particular day, I really didn't have time, but I made sure to call her. When I got to my hotel, I dialed her and she answered. Immediately, she began to share her frustration with me. Turns out, my girlfriend Asia had recently become the primary go-to for all of her mother's needs and her mother had become the primary source of her frustration.

Asia's mother, I learned, was a single woman of a certain age. She had always been cared for by her husband, and then, once he passed, her elderly mother stepped in. Then, the elderly mother passed away and this left Asia's mother for the first time with no one to care for her. Now, it is not unusual for adult children to take on the role reversal, but this was an extreme situation. Her mother had become reckless in her behavior. She became unwilling to step up on her own two feet. This, unfortunately, led to money issues, an unstable living situation, and a reckless drinking problem. So there I was, on a busy Friday night, lending a listening ear to a friend, and offering her words of encouragement.

If you see yourself in Asia's story, and if you've ever been in a compromising situation because of a loved one, please understand that everything is purposeful in life. The starting point of any issue, challenge, or difficulty is to realize that this situation has come into your life to teach you something about yourself. Nothing is a surprise to God. He knows all and He always has a word, an answer, and a solution. In this instance, God already told us what to do about family and friends in Timothy 5:8 "Anyone who does not provide for their relatives, and especially for their own household, has denied the faith and is worse than an unbeliever." So there's no question as to what we should do if we find ourselves in the position of primary caregiver. In fact, Asia's family was obedient to the Word by deciding to take care of her mother. Be careful not to say you love God whom you cannot see but yet, you have no love for the relative whom you see every day. Jesus commands us to help the weak, to provide for our relatives, and to cast all of our cares on Him. No matter how difficult it gets, have faith in God. He will sustain you.

I come to you Jehovah Nissi
(Exodus 17:15)

Thank you for life and thank you for being my God in the time of need. Lord, I am on the verge of an emotional meltdown. I am trying to help my [mother/father/sister/brother/child/friend]. You, God, are my God, and earnestly I will seek you. I thirst for you. My whole being longs for you, in a dry and parched land where there is no water. I have seen you in the sanctuary and beheld your power and your glory. I need you, Lord. God, I know you are in control and this issue [name the issue] is out of my hands but I need this to be well in my spirit. Lord, I need to be sober, not overly emotional. Lord, I need guidance on how to be a supporter when I need to support, and how to just listen when I need to listen. Lord help me to discern when I need to keep a healthy distance from certain relatives, and when I need to be readily available in cases of emergency. Lord, I love my [mother/father/sister/brother/child/friend] but I want your will to be done in [name the person] life. I believe you for victory, Lord. I declare and decree that you are God of the impossible. You wrote the end from the beginning and you are sovereign. Now God, I surrender this to situation to you. Touch [him/her] Lord with a fresh supply, restored health, a restored mind and a new spirit. I declare and decree that the weight is lifting right now. I love you, Lord. I thank you for hearing my cry. In Jesus' Name. Amen.

But if anyone does not provide for his relatives, and especially for members of his household, he has denied the faith and is worse than an unbeliever. – 1 Timothy 5:8

Humble yourselves, therefore, under the mighty hand of God so that at the proper time he may exalt you, casting all your anxieties on him, because he cares for you. – 1 Peter 5:6-7

Anxiety in a man's heart weighs him down, but a good word makes him glad. – Proverbs 12:25

In all things I have shown you that by working hard in this way we must help the weak and remember the words of the Lord Jesus, how he himself said, 'It is more blessed to give than to receive.' – Acts 20:35

Cast your burden on the Lord, and he will sustain you; he will never permit the righteous to be moved. – Psalm 55:22

48

A prayer for dating after divorce

> *"He has blinded their eyes and hardened their heart, lest they see with their eyes, and understand with their heart, and turn, and I would heal them."*
> **– John 12:40**

A FEW MONTHS AGO, I FOUND MYSELF ON THE PHONE WITH a friend who was having a very transparent moment. She was struggling with how to love after divorce, how to date after divorce, and how to manage life as a single parent.

Her greatest struggle had to do with a colleague who wanted to be more than a friend, but he wouldn't call it dating. Let's just say, it was a complicated "non relationship." There was so much drama and tension between them because he would play on her emotions one day, lead her on the next day, and then shut everything down by the weekend. This would happen on a consistent basis. But the most interesting thing about this scenario was that my friend was well aware of her role in the drama as well. In fact, prior to this dude showing up in her life, there was another guy whom she dated, but she didn't want him. She just used him to satisfy her own vacant space. The confession on her part eventually told a story of her challenges with men post-divorce. It just wasn't part of her life's blueprint to NOT be with a man, so of course, it was a place of heaviness.

Now I can somewhat relate to wanting to be in a relationship. I can even imagine the aches that must come with being a single mom after having been married. But I cannot comprehend being in a complicated non-relationship with a man who is anything less than kind, loving and respectful. I would never allow a man to share space with me if the space is not a loving space. *No ma'am. No Sir.* You teach people how to treat you by what you allow and what you don't allow; by how you care for yourself and how you show up in the room. All of that tells people around you what is acceptable and unacceptable. Being in a relationship is a choice. You get to decide whether you want to participate or not. And the tricky thing is relationships can be yummy but, there is a price to pay for sharing yourself with someone. I learned when I was married, not every moment of every day will be tulips and roses. Certainly, you will have to endure the good and the bad. But I believe that ultimately, life is about choices. You can choose to accept what has happened, or you can request better. If your life is filled with drama, tension and disregard, it's your responsibility to course correct. Ask for what you want. You get to rule and reign over your personal being until you submit to the covering of a mate by marriage.

So my two cents to my girlfriend was this: don't expect to attract what you want; you attract who you are. You won't attract greatness if you are ratchet. And if you ever happen to attract who you are not, respectfully bow out. Release the man back into the universe to find the right fit and to love and be loved as he deserves. No shade. Secondly, you deserve better. You are beautiful, smart, loving, and a uniquely valuable individual who is worthy of God's best even though you are divorced or a single mom. Nevertheless, you must resolve your issues. It is possible that if you have not been able to maintain a healthy, loving relationship, then you may be dealing with divorce residue. Divorce residue is unresolved issue that comes up post-divorce as a result of the divorce. If you don't handle it now, it will carry over into the next relationship. Until you resolve what worked and what didn't work, you will not be able to effectively move toward the love God has for you. You must do the work and get the lesson. Divorce came to teach you something. Learn it, and then wash off the residue. As you pray, run toward the nearest professional therapist you can find. That is how you come to terms with who you were then, who you are now, and who God created you to be.

I come to you God my Husband
(Isaiah 54:5)

Father, I come to you to say thank you for the privilege to call on you in this moment. While I am grateful for my life, I realize I am unsettled with being a divorced woman. I believe it was the right thing to do at the time, but I now struggle with the decision and the idea of being alone. I also have doubts sometimes about getting married again. Now that I have unloaded my truth to you, would you forgive me for any doubt or fear in my life that is not of you? I ask right now that you resolve my divorce residue. Help me to process out of my former marriage. Make it plain were I was wrong and teach me the lesson that I was supposed to learn from that relationship. Open my heart to receive course correction. Heal my heart. Touch my emotions, and build me up in you so that I will never again question my worth. Lord, I declare and decree that I am optimistic according to your word in Philippians. I will govern my thoughts and words and I declare and decree that I am whole, loveable and worthy of all that God has for me. I declare and decree that whatever status I desire, it will be. I declare and decree that whether I am divorced or married, I will be content in you and responsible with the man of God you send if/when you decide. Help me to love again and receive love. In Jesus' Name, Amen.

You shall not hate your brother in your heart, but you shall reason frankly with your neighbor, lest you incur sin because of him. – Leviticus 19:17

Strive for peace with everyone, and for the holiness without which no one will see the Lord. See to it that no one fails to obtain the grace of God; that no "root of bitterness" springs up and causes trouble, and by it many become defiled; – Hebrews 12:14-15

Therefore, if anyone is in Christ, he is a new creation. The old has passed away; behold, the new has come. – 2 Corinthians 5:17

Do not be deceived: "Bad company ruins good morals." – 1 Corinthians 15:33

Love is patient and kind; love does not envy or boast; it is not arrogant or rude. It does not insist on its own way; it is not irritable or resentful; it does not rejoice at wrongdoing, but rejoices with the truth. Love bears all things, believes all things, hopes all things, and endures all things. Love never ends. As for prophecies, they will pass away; as for tongues, they will cease; as for knowledge, it will pass away. – 1 Corinthians 13:4-8

49
A prayer for winning

> *"You shall remember the Lord your God, for it is he who gives you power to get wealth that he may confirm his covenant that he swore to your fathers, as it is this day."*
> **– Deuteronomy 8:18**

WHAT BOTHERS ME ABOUT THE COUNTRY THAT I LIVE in is that we are largely defined by status and our measures of success are limited to education, class, wealth, and material possessions. I'm so bothered by it that it has become the fuel and the fire behind my work. In my opinion, it is one of the biggest flaws in this country and it is the reason why we have so many issues. False definitions of success leave so many people confused. We've seen people steal and kill in order to keep up with the world standard. We've seen people take their own lives when they can't keep up. Furthermore, there is no class or course in primary education to help people learn what it truly means to be successful.

So if you have aspirations to win in life, let me share this with you. You don't have to accept the world's definition of success. You don't have to participate in the world system of winning and losing. You have to define success for yourself to get around this dilemma. Have you ever stopped to consider that you have the option to accept or reject any and everything that doesn't resonate with your belief system? Yes. The decision is yours and whoever told you that these were the rules and you had to play this game... were wrong. Whoever told you that the measure of success is attached to the highest levels of educational attainment, or what neighborhood you live in or how much you have in the bank, they told you wrong. The real measure of success for a believer is accomplishing the goal and the purpose for which God sent you here. God is not like man that He would endorse a world system that says you are a winner if you are educated, rich and powerful. In God's Kingdom, everyone is a winner--those with little and those with much. God does not show partiality (Acts 10:34.)

Winning is about accomplishing the primary goal and it is a goal that is not your own. Winning is not about pursuing your own agenda. Success is not measured by external things. Success at the end of the day will be measured by your pursuit of purpose. Does that mean that you shouldn't have your own personal goals and aspirations? Absolutely not. God is our source and supply. He is able to satisfy every need if you'd only ask Him. His word says to ask anything according to His will and it will be given (Mark 7:7.) Never put your own selfish desires above the pursuit of your God assignment. Pray that God would resolve this in your spirit and clarify your reasons for living. Pray for the courage to step out and follow God. Pray for the desire in your heart to line up with that which God has for you.

I come to you Jehovah-Shammah
(Ezekiel 48:35)

Father God in the name of Jesus, I come to lay before you my desire to win and to be successful in life. I want to evolve into the woman you have called me to be. God, would you please forgive me for putting my own needs and desires and wants before you? Lord, forgive me for what I did not know. Lord, help me to turn away from the world's definition of success. I accept right now that you are my standard. Therefore, I look to see and observe what you say, what you do and what I have received from your word according to Philippians 4:9. Your word says to ask for anything in your name and it will be given. So, I ask for you to guide me. Help me to put my life in order. Let my desires be your desires. I thank you right now for how far you've brought me. I'm believing you for greater. I declare victory and success over my life In Jesus' name, Amen.

Delight yourself in the Lord, and he will give you the desires of your heart. – Psalm 37:4

Do not be conformed to this world, but be transformed by the renewal of your mind, that by testing you may discern what is the will of God, what is good and acceptable and perfect. – Romans 12:2

For I know the plans I have for you, declares the Lord, plans for welfare and not for evil, to give you a future and a hope. – Jeremiah 29:11

This Book of the Law shall not depart from your mouth, but you shall meditate on it day and night, so that you may be careful to do according to all that is written in it. For then you will make your way prosperous, and then you will have good success. – Joshua 1:8

You shall remember the Lord your God, for it is he who gives you power to get wealth that he may confirm his covenant that he swore to your fathers, as it is this day. – Deuteronomy 8:18

50

A prayer now that you are saved

> *"Keep this Book of the Law always on your lips;*
> *meditate on it day and night, so that you may be*
> *careful to do everything written in it.*
> *Then you will be prosperous and successful."*
> **- Joshua 1:8**

IT WOULD REALLY BE NICE IF GETTING SAVED CAME WITH A step by step instruction guide on what to do NOW THAT YOU'RE SAVED. When I began to go deeper in my walk with the Lord, I found myself pouring over the word, searching the blue letter bible online and reading prayer books to sort through what I needed to know about God. I didn't feel overwhelmed by it all, but I did feel that there was just so much to learn and to know. The sweet thing is, I was hungry for more of his presence and thirsty to know his promises. So a few years ago, in my attempt to sort through it all, I wrote Scriptures on index cards. I was reaching for a structured way to learn the word and to apply it in my life. So on these index cards, I wrote in big letters what I thought to be the step-by-step fundamentals. Since starting that exercise, I have to admit: my life has never been the same. Those index cards did for me more than what I expected. They helped me to focus on a specific course of study, and they helped to increase my faith. It was a simple formula that worked. And still today, I have those index cards in the back of my purse journal.

If you're like me and you've come to a place in your life where you want to go deeper in your walk with God, then consider this: the more you seek the Lord, the better your life will become. It won't be without trials, but overall your worst day with God will be better than your best day without Him. If you have a natural pull towards a specific passage of scripture, then follow that. In addition to that, I'm going to give you just of a few of my index cards for consideration and prayer. I believe they will help you with your faith walk during the beginning, middle, and end of your journey.

- **Faith** – first focus on your faith because it is impossible to move in the word of God if you don't believe in God. Study Hebrews 11:1 Hebrews 11:6 and Romans 10:17 and Mark 9:23.
- **Prayer** – one would think you'd start with prayer. However, faith causes your prayer to work. Prayer does not cause your faith to work. So start with faith and then focus on prayer. Mark 9:23, John 5:14, John 14:13
- **Success** – I found it very encouraging to focus on the promises of God for a good life. The promises that I focused on were words about success and prosperity: Deuteronomy 28:1-14 and Joshua 18 Also, read Romans 12:2, Deuteronomy 11:18, Philippians 2:5, and Joshua 1:8.

I come to you Jehovah-Tsidkenu
(Jeremiah 23:6)

Father God in the name of Jesus, I thank you for hearing my prayers. I confess I believe in you and I believe that Jesus died so that I could be saved and all my sins forgiven. Thank you for thinking enough of me to create a plan for my life. God this is all new for me and I'm looking for direction. I'm asking you to guide me toward the right tools and resources. I thank you in advance for the index cards and the assistance you will provide. I want to get this right, but I admit it can be overwhelming at times. Please hear my prayer and direct me to a local church. I pray now for the church and the shepherd. I pray for ministry leaders and those who might be assigned to me in the process. I believe you're working all things together for my good and nothing but great things will come out of my pursuit of you. Now God, do it according to your will. Stretch me, grow me, and hold my hand as I take this trip in Jesus' name, Amen.

Do not conform to the pattern of this world, but be transformed by the renewing of your mind. Then you will be able to test and approve what God's will is--his good, pleasing and perfect will. – Romans 12:2

Therefore, if anyone is in Christ, he is a new creation. The old has passed away; behold, the new has come. – 2 Corinthians 5:17

Do your best to present yourself to God as one approved, a worker who has no need to be ashamed, rightly handling the word of truth. – 2 Timothy 2:15

But now you must also rid yourselves of all such things as these: anger, rage, malice, slander, and filthy language from your lips. – Colossians 3:8

All Scripture is breathed out by God and profitable for teaching, for reproof, for correction, and for training in righteousness. – 2 Timothy 3:16

51
A prayer declaration for women

> *"The tongue has the power of life and death,*
> *and those who love it will eat its fruit."*
> **– Proverbs 18:21**

NOTHING SHIFTED MY LIFE LIKE DISCOVERING PSALM 139, which affirms this truth: we are all here by God's design, on purpose for a purpose. It's just like God to cancel any doubt about whether or not His children are here by accident. Isn't it sweet to know you are not an accident under whatever circumstances that transpired between your mother and father? Beyond that, God has a plan for your life and an earmark for you to have a rich and rewarding life. How you take hold of the abundant life God has for you is by exercising your faith, authority and power through the declaration of what you say. I encourage you to read these declarations every day or find just one that resonates with you. Be intentional about speaking these words into the atmosphere daily.

I declare and decree I am a child of the most high God. I am a daughter of the king and an heiress to the throne.

I declare and decree it is in You, God that I have my living, my breathing and my being

I declare and decree I am here on purpose for a purpose and my life matters according to Psalms 139

I declare and decree God has a good plan for my life according to Jeremiah 29:11

I declare and decree life and death is in the power of my tongue

I declare and decree I am healthy, whole, and well

I declare and decree my relationships are healthy, loving and supportive

I declare and decree the work of my hands is blessed and everything I touch will prosper

I declare and decree favor in my work, job, career and business

I declare and decree I am celebrated wherever I go

I declare and decree my gift is making room for me

I declare and decree I am a winner and I come from a bloodline of champions

I declare and decree God is the source and the supplier of all my needs

I declare and decree the universe is rearranging itself for my best interest

The Lord is my strength, my standard, and my banner, my redeemer and this is my prayer I surrender it in Jesus' Name. Amen

So is my word that goes out from my mouth: It will not return to me empty, but will accomplish what I desire and achieve the purpose for which I sent it. – Isaiah 55:11

You will also decree a thing, and it will be established for you; and light will shine on your ways. – Job 22:28

And all things, whatever you shall ask in prayer, believing, you shall receive. – Matthew 21:22

May he give you the desire of your heart and make all your plans succeed. – Psalm 20:4

Take delight in the LORD, and he will give you the desires of your heart. – Psalm 37:4

52
A prayer resolve
for women

> "*Let no corrupting talk come out of your mouths,*
> *but only such as is good for building up, as fits the*
> *occasion, that it may give grace to those who hear.*"
> – *Ephesians 4:29*

THERE IS A FORMULA FOR WINNING IN LIFE. GOD HAS A PLAN to prosper you. His word says I've come to that you might have life and have it the full. The formula includes believing in God and believing Him. You must take God at his word, receive His promises and then begin to speak forth positive words. I encourage you to read this resolve every day or find just one that resonates with you and be intentional about placing your resolve in the atmosphere daily.

1. I, a woman of this world, resolve to support and celebrate each women.

2. I, a woman of this world, resolve to stop and listen to the wise words of those here to teach me something.

3. I, a woman of this world, resolve to silence the incoming traffic so I can hear the voice of God directing and guiding me.

4. I, a woman of this world, resolve to pay forward that which I have graciously received but didn't earn or deserve.

5. I, a woman of this world, resolve I will not use expletives to speak to or about each other women.

6. I, a woman of this world, resolve to stop showing up out of order in the name of fame.

7. I, a woman of this world, resolve to invest more in myself than I spend on myself.

8. I, a woman of this world, resolve to stop creating demand and start creating supply.

9. I, a woman of this world, resolve to take better care of my health and wellness out of respect for the body God gave me.

10. I, a woman of this world, resolve to give more, love more, do more and be more.

11. I, a woman of this world, resolve to stop playing super woman and neglecting my personal aspirations, goals and dreams.

12. I, a woman of this world, resolve to stop judging and start accepting cultural, ethnic, social, economic, and religious differences of others.

13. I, a woman of this world, resolve to never give up on believing in equality.

14. I, a woman of this world, resolve to discover my purpose on earth and move into the space I am called to serve.

15. I, a woman of this world, resolve to be a good steward our time, talent and resources.

16. I, a woman of this world, resolve to do my part take a stand for equality.

17. I, a woman of this world, resolve to be an example for others.

18. I, a woman of this world, resolve to do better, be better, and live greater so I can go higher.

19.   I, a woman of this world, resolve to engage in the political process to support laws that are for the best interest of all people .

20.   I, a woman of this world, resolve to use my plat- form for good—to uplift, inspire, encourage, motivate, challenge and support women higher.

Whoever guards his mouth preserves his life; he who opens wide his lips comes to ruin. – Proverbs 13:3

Know this, my beloved brothers: let every person be quick to hear, slow to speak, slow to anger; – James 1:19

Let no corrupting talk come out of your mouths, but only such as is good for building up, as fits the occasion, that it may give grace to those who hear. – Ephesians 4:29

So is my word that goes out from my mouth: It will not return to me empty, but will accomplish what I desire and achieve the purpose for which I sent it. – Isaiah 55:11

You will also decree a thing, and it will be established for you; and light will shine on your ways. – Job 22:28

53
About the Author

DEE MARSHALL IS A SOUGHT-AFTER INTERNATIONAL speaker, certified Coach, author and TV Lifestyle Personality, Dee Marshall is CEO of DeeMarshalletc.com, Founder at Girlfriends Pray Ministries international ministry of over 200K women. The ministry recently celebrated their 5th year anniversary with expansion kick-off in Bermuda and now the 501(c)3 not-for-profit is in over twenty-five US markets in seventeen states and four countries. Having been covered by numerous media outlets to include ABC, MSNBC, Fox, WMAR, WATC, Praise 102.5, 98.7 Kiss, Black Enterprise Magazine, Essence Magazine, Upscale, ShePreneur, Rolling Out, Gospel Today and Heart & Soul Magazine and featured as the resident Life Coach on TV One Makeover Manor she is a renowned expert on personal transformation for women.

As a result of her service to women, she has received numerous awards. She was selected as Hope Magazine Top 25 Women that Inspires alongside many powerful women from around the globe including Michelle Obama, Oprah Winfrey, Kerry Washington, Princess Kate, Karen Bass, Tasha Cobbs, Hilary Clinton.

Other recognition awards include Who's Who New York City, NAACP Award, New Brunswick Education Fund Hall of Distinguished Alumni, National Association of Female Executives Women in Corporate Award and many more.

Marshall resides in the New York metro area with her furry baby Sophie and there she is working on a new initiative with The White House Council for Women and Girls. Contact Dee Marshall at www.GirlfriendsPray.org Connect online @DeeCMarshall

54
About
Girlfriends Pray

Girlfriends Pray is one of the fastest growing ministries for women of faith!

Our ministry was birthed to encourage, inspire, motivate, and empower women through prayer. Founded on 1 Thessalonians 5:17, our mission is to get more women od for using a few ordinary women to do the extraordinary work of getting one million women around the world united in prayer.

Girlfriends Pray is our primary prayer service which convenes five days a week at 7am and 10pm EST and at noon via teleconference line.

Girlfriends Pray Mid-Week is our mid-week, mid-day prayer service which convenes Wednesdays at noon EST via teleconference line.

Girlfriends Pray/Amigas Pray is a dedicated prayer service for Latina (Spanish-speaking) women of faith on Wednesday nights at 10 pm EST via teleconference.

Girlfriends Pray Local consists of our live and in-person groups led by GP Ambassadors who convene regularly for fellowship, food, and meaningful discussion about prayer.

Girlfriends Pray Life Camp provides abundant living resources for women committed to their spiritual growth and personal development.

Connect with us @GirlfriendsPray #GirlfriendsPray www. GirlfriendsPray.org

56555558R00173

Made in the USA
Lexington, KY
24 October 2016